THE

WARS OF THE RAJAS,

BEING THE

HISTORY OF ANANTAPURAM.

THE

WARS OF THE RAJAS,

BEING THE

HISTORY OF ANANTAPURAM.

WRITTEN IN TELUGU; IN OR ABOUT THE YEARS

1750-1810

TRANSLATED INTO ENGLISH,

BY

CHARLES PHILIP BROWN

OF THE MADRAS CIVIL SERVICE
TELUGU TRANSLATOR TO GOVERNMENT
SENIOR MEMBER OF THE COLLEGE BOARD, ETC

KALPAZ

ISBN: 978-93-5128-811-4(HB)

First Published in 1853
Indian Reprint in 2017

Published by

Kalpaz Publications
C-30, Satyawati Nagar,
Delhi – 110052
E-mail: kalpaz@hotmail.com
Website: kalpazpublications.com
Ph.: +91-9212142040

PREFACE.

In examining those manuscripts collected by Colonel Mackenzie, which are preserved in the College Library at Madras, I found several historical volumes written in Telugu, Kannadi and Marata. A few of these are interesting, as showing the condition of the country during the last years of the Hindu or Musulman dominion. One of these tales is published in the present small volume: another in the History of Hyder and Tippoo written in Marata: which I translated and published a few years since. I have several more such tracts ready for publication.

Those who are learning Telugu, and Natives who study English, will find these histories useful in attaining the style used in business.

I have divided these narratives into Chapters and Sections: but in the original there areno such divisions.

After perusing my Telugu Dialogues and part of my Telugu Reader, the student may undertake the present volume: the publications hitherto in vogue may be safely laid aside. They are three: commonly known as the Vicramarca Stories, Punchatantra Tales, and Teloogoo Selections. The first two are unworthy of perusal. The third is better, but is entirely needless to those who possess the Telugu Dialogues and Telugu Reader.

C. P. BROWN.

TRANSLATION OF THE

TELUGU HISTORIES AND TALES.

THE WARS OF THE RA'JAS.

THE ANNALS OF HANDEH ANANTAPURAM.

CHAPTER FIRST.

1. While Bucca Rayalu ruled Vidyānagar [Vijayanagar] on the banks of the Pampa, his chief servant Chikkappa Wadeyar in the SS. year 1286 answering to "Krodhi" [A.D. 1364] built a lake: it was near Devaraconda, in the province of Nandela: south of Vidyanagar. He saw the river Pandu, which rises in the Cambu-giri-swami hills: at Devaraconda he stopped it with an embankment and thus formed a lake*: at the two (marava) outlets of which he built two villages. The one at the eastern (marava) mouth he named Bucca Raya's Sea [also called Bucca Samudram; about 50 miles South East of Bellary]; thus naming it after his lord. And the village at the western mouth he named, after his lady, Ananta-Sagaram [also called Handeh Ananta Puram]. He also observed the river Chitravati which rises in the hill sacred to Vencateswara, lord of Varagiri, in the Elamanchi country, sixteen miles South of Bucca Raya Samudram: here also he built a lake. And at each end of the bank he built a village. The one at the east end he called Bucca Patnām; and the western village he named Ananta Sagaram [also called Kotta Cheruvu, or "New-Tank"]. At this place Chiccappa Wadayar departed this life.

---

* On the map this appears in N. Lat. 14° 45, and 77, 38 East.

2. After some time (a) this lake, called Bucca Raya Samudram became so full of water that the two (maravas) sluices did not suffice, and were rushing in a flood. When the (āyagāndlu) petty village officers and the townsmen came and beheld this, a [goddess] possessed a woman: and she exclaimed I am Ganga-Bhavāni. If you will feed me with a human sacrifice, I will stop here: if not I will not stop.

While (1) the villagers* and the elders took counsel about making the sacrifice, (9) Ganga Devi possessed (8) a girl, (7) not yet grown up, named Musalamma; she was the (6) seventh and (5) youngest daughter-in-law of (4) Basi Reddi (3) who dwelt (2) at Bukka Raya Samudram: [the goddess (11) said to her] (10) Become thou the sacrifice.

She accordingly was prepared to become a sacrifice; she adorned herself [as a bride] with yellow and red paint: wearing a pure vest and holding a lime in her hand. She set out [in procession] from [her] home, and came up on the embankment. She adored the feet of her father-in-law, Basi Reddi, and did homage to the townsfolk. She said I have received the commands of Ganga-Bhavāni: "I am going to become a sacrifice." Thirty feet from the "Embassy, sluice" there was now (gummada) a gap: between which and the bank a chasm had opened. She went through the chasm and stood therein:† and they poured in earth and stones upon her (lit. upon the bank): so the bank stood [firm and safe].‡

3. The following day this Musalamma who had thus become§ a sacrifice, possessed the females of the village: she said "Make a

(a) Page 2.

* The numerals here placed shew how the words are arranged in the original.

† Literally, by her going and standing.

‡ This is one of many stories that go to prove the rite of human sacrifices in ancient days. Among bramins such practices have always been denounced as crimes: but the local petty deities or *pariar gods* are honoured by slaughtering goats instead of human sacrifices, to this day.

§ Such a sacrifice, as also the burning alive of a widow, was always represented as a voluntary and meritorious suicide.

stone image of me, place it under a tree, and worship it." Accordingly they erected it, and worship her: but there is no chapel.

Besides, if people who passed this way or that way near the breach cried out "Musalamma" she used to reply "Ho!" But one day in the evening* as men went for grass, and called to her in the same manner, she answered. On hearing her, they replied, though thou art dead thou art still proud. From that time she never answers. From that day [Saint] Musalamma is worshipped.

Villages as great as this Bucca Raya Samudram and Anantapuram: and lakes as great as these, are no where else to be seen.†

4. Afterwards (ª) Krishna Rayalu a descendant of Bucca Raya ruled Vidyanagar; and he died in the Salivahana Sacam year 1487‡ named Krodhana [A. D. 1565] on Sunday, the sixth day of the bright fortnight in the month Jyeshtha.§

His wives were two, named Chinna Devi and Tirumala Devi: as they had only female children, Tirumala Devi's daughter was married to Rama Rayalu: and Chinna Devi's daughter was given in marriage to his younger brother Tirumala Rayalu.

Then these ladies [the queens dowager] proposed to crown Rama Raya as "Son-in-law Regnant."‖

5. There was one Salacam¶ Timmaiia who was a (golla) treasurer of the household: he saw that the country was in confusion; as the

---

* Lit. One day at night.

† Thus far the Introduction: which the learner may omit for the present because it may in some places appear intricate.

(ª) Page 3.

‡ *Aguneti* is, "corresponding to."—The manuscript states 1387 but this is clearly an error: for that year is not Krodhana, and is long before the well known era of Krishna Rayalu.

§ This prince's death is sometimes misdated in the year Tarana, SS. 1387 that is, A.D. 1464. But the petty ruler who died on that day is some other raja of whom nothing certain is known.

‖ Lit. they conferred the Aliya-pattam. "The word Aliya in Kannadi signifies a son-in-law." Pattam is installation.

¶ In Telugu and Kannadi, the family name stands first: thus we should say Timmaiia of the Salacam family.

treasury was in his hands, he seduced the host* of the four arms. He wished to seize and imprison (the sons-in-law) Rama Raya and Tirumala Raya. On hearing these tidings they fled the country and betook themselves to the Penugonda country, where they raised some troops and marched to A'davani [Adhoni, a town north east of Bellary.] There they dwelt four months : and collected more troops in the Candanul† and Gadwal and thereabouts, then they came, with forces of every arm, to attack [the usurper] at Vidyanagar. [A. D. 1563.]

Salacam Timmanna was informed of these matters by his spies. He requested the aid of [the four Turkish chieftains] Kutb Shāh, Farīd Shāh, Nizam Shāh and Ali Adal Shah.‡ He wrote letters to them and to others, saying if you will come with a well equipped army, I will deliver all this kingdom into your hands.

6. They read [his letters] and accordingly came with all their hosts and halted within two miles of Vidyānagar.

When Rama Raya and Tirumala Raya heard of this they summoned Handeh Hanumappa Nayudu [a well known chieftain], celebrated as a warrior, who dwelt at Sonnalāpuram : they enlisted him in their employ, with his troops. They went and halted on the bank of the Tungabhadra§ two leagues from Vidyanagar. This place being new to the troops of those 'Pachas' [the Musulman chieftains] they appointed Salacam Timmanna's army to go in front, and prepared for a battle.

7. Rama Raya(a) and Tirumala Raya heard of this. They sounded the alarm of war in open daylight, and fell upon Salacam Timmanna's host which was before their face. The soldiers of his host said, This fellow is a (golla||) herdsman : being rich he has attempted to usurp dominion. If we aid him the divine aid cannot be grant-

---

* Chaturanga balam denotes a host of four kinds : horse, foot, elephants and chariots. Hence the name for chess.

† Called Kurnool in the maps.

‡ Compare Hamilton's Gazetteer under the name Beedur.

§ Toombuddra of the Maps.

(a) Page 4.

|| Golla is the proper name of the cow-keeper-caste : but also is the name of those men who are employed as transporters of treasure.

ed us. So they quitted the battle-field. Salacam Timmaya was taken prisoner and lost his life.

8. The ladies heard this news: they called their (pradhan) ministers and ordered that Rama Raya and Tirumala Raya should be called: and that the government should be committed to them. The servants (pradhan) accordingly went forward to meet them, brought them home and committed the city to their charge.

9. Afterwards, Rama Raya and Tirumala Raya took counsel about opposing the (Pachas) Mahomedan chieftains in war. They parted the forces in town and their own troops, into three bodies: they called Handeh Hanumappa Nayadu [chief] of Sonnalapuram, and said: thou art a very brave man: we will give thee some troops. Array these with the troops now in thy hand and march against Nizam Shah. Attack him: if thou conquer him, as much as thy heart fancies shall be bestowed [on thee.] So saying they gave him some troops and sent him: while Rama Raya led some troops against Kutb Shah: and Tirumal Rayalu marched with his own troops against Farīd Shah. A great battle took place. The ("Padshahs") Turks could not stand their ground, and were routed.

10. Hande Hanumappa Nayudu having the Nizam prisoner, came and offered him as a present to Rama Raya and Tirumala Raya. Hereupon they were very gracious to him: they applauded him and desired Hande Hanumappa Nayudu to state what he wished.* He replied, Whatever your honours please: it will be equal to all rewards.

Thereupon they bestowed upon him, in the eastern country, Nandela, Bucca Raya Samudram, and Dharmavaram, and Kanicallu.(a) Also, in the west, Ballari, and Kārgōdu; these villages, with [complimentary] titles. Then this Hande Hanumappa Nayudu took leave of the Rajas, and went to Nandela: where he arrived in the year SS. 1491 [A. D. 1569] of which the title is Sucla, in the month Margasira. / After taking charge of office,† he proceeded to Bucca Raya Samudram where he beheld the lake, and learning how

---

* Lit. what is in thy mind.

(a) Page 5.

† Lit: after inquiring into the affairs of the district.

great it was, he caused a (nagar) royal residence to be built before the fort in the village: around which he erected a bastion and governed the realm. In the year SS. 1505 entitled Chitrabhan (A. D. 1582) he died.

11. Then his son Immadi Hampā Nayudu was placed on his throne. From the year SS. 1506 entitled Swabhanu (A. D. 1583) until SS. 1518 titled Manmatha (A. D. 1595) he ruled the realm and he died at Bukka Raya Samudram.

12. While his son Malacappa Nayudu was ruling, Sri Ranga Rayalu (the son of Tirumala Raya ruler of Vidyānagar,) proceeded towards Chandragiri with a view to survey (i. e. rule) his realm. Then the army of the Pacha again marched from the north to seize Vidyānagar: and halted in Kalyanam and Kalburgi and thereabouts. When Sri Ranga Rayalu heard these tidings he rapidly returned to Vidyānagar, and then marched with his army towards Kalyanam and Kalburgi. He summoned Malacappa Nayudu, (who was at Bucca Samudram) with his troops and taking him along with him fought and routed [the Turks].

13. Afterwards, this Malacappa Nayudu took leave of the Rayalu and built a town anew, at Bucca Raya Samudram, and reigned until the year Vicari [A. D. 1599]. Then those [Turkish] Pachas again marched with their armies and warred against Vidyānagar. In this battle Sri Ranga Rayalu not being able to stand his ground was taken prisoner by them.(*) The pachas beginning at Penugonda, conquered all the country, and ruled it.

Afterwards this Malacappa Nayudu on hearing what had happened to Sri Ranga Rayalu, said, The Turks have become mighty: it is not good for us hereafter to take any steps against them. So he betook himself to the Pachas, and behaved obediently in their service. So they had great favour to him: they bestowed on him the lands formerly granted by the old Rajahs, and Buccapatnam in the Elemanchi country, and Ananta Sagaram: these two towns with the hamlets under them, and also the title "Padshah Vazir" (Royal Minister).

14. Afterwards this Malacappa Nayudu dwelt at Bucca Raya Samudram, and sorrowed because that by reason of his dwelling

---

(*) Page 6.

here he had no male offspring. One day he went with his (sawāri) train to Ananta Sagaram and visited Ella Reddi* the descendant of Chinnapa Reddi: who said my lord [i. e. your lordship] is come, let him [i. e. Please to] come to our house and accept the *tāmbūlam*†." Accordingly [Malacappa Nayudu] went to their house, and seeing that it was prolific,‡ he said surely were I to build my palace here, I should have offspring." So thinking in his heart, he at that time accepted the tāmbūlam, returned to Bucca Raya Samudram, where he told this matter to his wives. Next day he sent for Ella Reddi and said§ I want the place you dwell in: favour me with it. " He replied what great matter is it to bestow your place upon yourself: Please to come."

15. Then [Malacappa Nayudu] bestowed a vest and the *tāmbūlam* [as gifts] on Ella Reddi and sent him home. After ten days more had passed [Malacappa Nayudu] caused a mansion to be built on the spot where Ella Reddi's house had stood, and dwelt there. From that time this village has been named Hande Anantapuram. [His family name being Handeh.]

Then Ella Reddi and his people pulled down the sluice which stood at a quarter of an hour's distance without the fort, and built a (new) sluice at a quarter-hour distance further on. They raised a bank where the former sluice had stood, and caused a house and a market to be built on the spot and dwelt there.‖

16. After some time (a) this Malacappa Nayudu's principal wife¶ Siddha Ramamma bore four sons named Devappa N. and Chinna Ramappa N. and Niçça-mada Lingappa N. and Hampa Nayudu. Afterwards Malacappa N. divided his realm thus. To his eldest son Devappa N. he gave the Nandela lands in the east.

---

* The old rulers of the Telugu country were denominated Reddis or Chief Farmers. Their dominion lasted from A. D. 1250 until A. D. 1498 when they all fell under the dominion of the Musalmans.

† Paun-leaf, offered in homage to a guest.

‡ *Santāna vriddhi-caram:* probably meaning that it was full of children.

§ Lit: they said.

‖ [This passage in the Telugu is obscure.]

(a) Page 7.

¶ Paṭṭapu Bharya is in fact the wife alone; literally the crowned wife. In such passages N denotes " Nayudu."

To the second son Chinna Ramappa N. he gave Ballāri and Curugodu.

To the third, named Niçça-mada Lingappa N. he gave the Candup-pa and Kanicallu districts.

To the fourth son Hampa Nayudu he gave Anantapuram, Bucca-sāgaram, Buccapatnam and Dharmavaram. Thus did Hande Malacappa N. divide [his realm] and each of them governed his own lands.* After a short time in the year Siddharti, SS. 1542 (A. D. 1619) [Malacappa Nayudu] closed his days.

17. Afterwards his fourth son Hampa N. ruled Anantapuram and the other towns until his death in the year Prajotpatti. SS. 1554 (A. D. 1631.)

His son Prasanna Siddappa N. was crowned in the SS. year Angirasa (A. D. 1632.) and ruled until his decease in the year Vicari, SS. 1582. (A. D. 1659.)

His son Pavādappa N. ruled as his father had done and closed his days in the year SS. 1593 Virodhicrit. [A. D. 1671.]

18. At that time Peda Timmappa N. of Raidurgam, placed a garrison in Dharmavaram, and dwelt there.

As Pavadappa N's son Siddappa was a boy four years old, his mother Sidda Ramamma carried on the rule in his name.†

At this time the Mayana,‡ Nabob of Karpa (Cuddapa) came [to Anantapuram] with his whole army, in order to recover the tribute money due to him for four years from the year Paridhavi. SS. 1595 (A. D. 1672) and encamped at the distance of one (coss) league. He sent his messenger and said, Either give me the [tribute] money, or the realm.(*) When the herald delivered this message [the lady] Sidda Ramamma on hearing it, took her son Siddappa Nayudu and visited the Mayana Nabob and obtained a release from the tribute: she then took leave and returned to Hande Anantapuram.

---

* Lit: They were ruling their their places.

† Literally, setting the boy before her. That is, acting on his behalf.

‡ This personage is usually styled the Mayāna: his full title was Nawab Mayana Abdul Halim Khan. He is sometimes called Halim Khan or Abdul Halim Khan, or the Karpa Nabob.

(*) Page 8.

Afterwards, [her son] this Siddappa N. ruled the land until SS. 1619 [A. D. 1696] the year Dhatu, when he ended his days at Anantapuram.

19. His sons were Prasannappa N. and Pavādappa N. Of these two the eldest Prasannappa N. was crowned in SS. 1620 [A. D. 1697] the year Iswara: and ruled the land until the year Manmatha SS. 1637 [misprinted 1633] (which is A. D. 1715.) when the Nabob, Mayana Mōchē Mīyān (the Subedar of Karpa) marched to Rāyadurgam, and besieged a village thereunto attached named Būdigumma. He sent orders to Prasannappa Nayudu to join him, bringing his own troops. On reading the command, Prasannappa Nayudu wished to go to the army; and therefore appointed a man of the Balje, [caste] named Siriappa to keep Anantapuram [during his absence.] He said to Siriappa, "keep one eye on the realm, and one on the lake. As the lake did not fill* I have dug (talipera calvalu) feeding channels, and have led the water on to the black land in the lake, and have carried on rice cultivation on the (goçulu) lowlands† and it has turned out well. You must tend it carefully." After saying these words he departed with his troops. This Siriappa carried on the government in conformity with these orders. In the year Vicari SS. 1641 (A. D. 1719) in the month Chaitra, on the fifth day of the wane, there was an unseasonable shower, and the lake was somewhat filled.

20. On the 8th day of the wane in the month Vaisakh of this year, it again rained and there was a prodigious flood, so that both the sluices were rushing at the full: on the east side a breach formed, and another was burst in the west bank. Siriappa wrote tidings of this to his [master] Prasannappa N. who on reading([a]) the letter informed the Nabob [Mōchē Miyān.] Then he left some troops there under the command of Hali Nayak and he himself returned home speedily and arrived at Kūdēru. When Siriappa heard of this, he said "There is no knowing what punishment Master will inflict [on

---

* The original correctly is చెరువు నిండనందున *nindunanduna* "as it did not fill." Not understanding the passage the native who copied it wrote *nindiunnanduna* నిండియున్నందున "as it did fill."

† The words *talipera* and *goçulu* are local phrases. The tank being dry, he watered it by means of canals.

([a]) Page 9.

me] and through fear he caused booths to be erected at the two places where the breaches happened: he summoned the farmers, carnams (clerks) and people from both villages, and [labouring] by day and night he caused grass, earth, and stone to be cast into the breaches, and was thus securing the dyke of the lake. Next day Prasannappa Nayudu came from Kūdēru to Rāçānapallē, and sent word that in four hours he* would arrive.

As he was accordingly coming along the bank of the lake he enquired whether Siriappa was well. As he drew near the breaches, Siriappa, losing all courage, fell down on the spot where he stood, struggled, and died.

When Prasannappa N. heard of this, he laid out some money on his funeral: he himself did not proceed to Anantapuram, but pitched his tent close by, and dwelt there night and day. He caused the two breaches to be closed, and appeased [the gods with offerings] and was then thinking of going into town.

CHAPTER SECOND.

1. Meantime, his lady Siddamma had borne him a son named Ramappa N. and the boy was four years old; when two courtezans named Vasantamma and Laççamma came from Tādimarri to Anantapuram: they subsisted by their usual employ; the people of the village used to go into the (nagari) palace to receive [their dole of] milk and buttermilk, for their children. This (miss) Vasantamma went also into the fort for buttermilk; when Prasannappa Nayudu beholding her face([a]) and figure, fell in love with her; he said "whose [child] are you?" She said, "I am a courtezan:" and told him all her story:† whereupon he said "Stay here with me." He allotted her a separate dwelling close by the palace: he supplied her with food and clothing: he was unable to be away from this Vasantamma even for a moment: and even when he went in procession‡ to Bucca-

---

* Lit. Saying I will come.

([a]) Page 10.

† Lit: by (her) telling.

‡ Swāri i. e. sawāri, procession.

raya Samudram he would carry her along with him, and return with her: [and] he [still] lodged on the bank of the lake.

Such being the state of things, this Vasantamma's elder sister Laççamma seeing that his lordship kept her younger sister in his palace, feared lest some harm might happen [to herself, the eldest.] She therefore set out and went to Tādimarri, and took* up her abode with Pedda Tirumala Nayudu, the baron of that place.

2. She sent a message to her younger sister Vasantamma saying, "It is not well for thee to be thus in the hands of strangers. If thou wilt come to me, thou mayest live at liberty. You should gather together money where you are, and by any contrivance flee from bondage, escape, and come." So saying she was carrying on fraud under hand.

This Vasantamma sent [an answer, telling] the following plan to her elder sister. If thou wilt take some troops and set out and come to Anantapuram, to pay a visit to Vencateswara [the god at] Devaraçonda, I also will obtain permission from my lord and come as thou proposest, to that place. She sent a letter in reply to this effect.

Then, accordingly, this Laççamma came to that place with troops: she placed some of them in ambush near Pasuluru, a village in the Tadimarri district, a league from Devaraconda: while with a moderate attendance she arrived at Devaraconda.

On hearing this news Vasanta said to Prasannappa Nayudu, "My eldest sister Laççamma has come to visit [the god] Vencateswara who lives at Devaraconda: I have not for many days had a sight of her, and I therefore wish to go there and see her and to visit the god, and return here in the evening." So saying she earnestly intreated him; Prasannapa Nayu gave her a guard and sent her, saying Go quickly and return in the evening.

3. So Vasanta(a) set out: and after she had gone a little way Prasannapa Nayudu suspected something: he again sent ten men from hence, and called her back and said "After we [that is, *I*] have returned home to the village [from this tent at the lake] we will send some people to guard you." He persuaded her and stopped her that day. But a doubt arose in her mind, "Surely somebody has gone and told his

---

* Lit: Having arrived.

(a) Page 11.

honour something or other: if I go (home) into the fort I shall not have the opportunity of joining my sister."

That night while Prasannapa N. was sleeping she took all the wealth that were there, and tying the things on her middle and on her thighs to conceal them, she put her petticoat over all. Then she drew the dagger* that lay on the bed, and cut the throat of this Prasannapa Nayudu: and while she was going along wishing to make her escape, being unable to see, she was going here and there [in the dark.]

4. At that moment the guards who were around the tent of the baron, and the (Dalavai) commandant Hālī Nayudu and the rest, lighted a torch and went into the tent. They saw that his honour was at his last gasp: and that Miss Vasanta had come out of the tent to make her escape. They called her in, and on asking who had done this deed, Prasannapa Nayudu, who was at his last gasp, made a sign with his hand, pointing at Vasantamma. They called for the waiting women, had her searched, and these women having detected the bags of things, took them from her, brought and laid them before the commandant and the others.

5. Afterwards, they seized Miss Vasanta and pinioned her and put her in confinement. They wrote a letter telling the tidings to Prasannapa Nayu's younger brother Pavādapa N. who was at Buccapatnam. On reading the letter he instantly set out from thence and came to the bank of the lake: then he placed Vasantamma in the fort, and built a wall around her, within which she ended her days.

Thus Prasannapa Nayu died the same day in the year Vicari SS. 1641 (A. D. 1719.)

6. Afterwards, (*) from the year Sarvari, SS. 1642 (A. D. 1720) this Pavādapa Nayu ruled the land. There were three captains (Foujdars) named Sardār Khan, and Alli Khan, and Mohammad Khan. These three marching with a small force, by this route to Pedda Sirigiri from the Mayana Nabob of Kadapa, halted within half a coss of Anantapuram, on the brink of the river at Zūṭūr.

---

* This story resembles that of Judith and Holophernes.

(*) Page 12.

When Pavadapa Nayu heard this news, there was with him a man named Rāmāji, the (vakīl) minister of the Kadapa Nabob. By this man's hand he sent (Kānuka) a peace offering to [those chieftains.] They questioned Rāmāji regarding the news of the place, and he replied, "This Pavadapa Nayu is a mere [Kaif dār] drunkard, and here is no proper management. If you propose visiting his honour I will go and tell Pavadapa Nayu* and will call you into [the fort.] After you enter and have had an interview [you must say] "The tribute due by your house is now three or four years in arrear, and accordingly our Master has commanded saying:—

7. "If you pay the money, well: or else you may come along with us." If you express yourselves thus, and seat his honour;† from that time the place will be in your power." Such were the treacherous counsels he gave: then he took leave of them, and returned into the fort. There he spoke to Pavadapa Nayu‡ saying "The commanders of the force are eager to visit you, and have sent messengers from them [to you,] along with me. They are respectable men: you should invite them in, and compliment them with robes of honour and the tambūlam [or paun leaf,] give them an audience, and dismiss them. This will be very profitable to our future business."

The [laird] assented, and said If they come in with a few [followers]§ we will admit them. [Then Ramaji said to the messengers,] Go and bring them in. Thus he spoke to the vakeels and sent them away. They went and invited the (faujdars) commandants, and placed them in the (meda) upper chamber. Then they gave notice of this to Pavadapa Nayudu.

8. [Pavadapa Nayu] came to receive them in the marble‖ hall, and having called them out of the (meda) upper chamber, they had an interview in the (padasala) inner hall. They asked of each others health,¶

* Variki is the respectful phrase: literally To them: meaning To his honour.

† In demanding money they sometimes make the debtor sit down and forbid his arising until the demand is satisfied.

‡ Variki, to them: that is to his honour, to him.

§ Lit: if they come moderately, we will in like manner give an interview.

‖ Lit. The plaister hall or court.

¶ Lit: of their health and wealth.

and he said I will send a dinner(a)and baths,&c. for you from the palace.* He therefore sent them to the (meda) house. That day they dwelt in the upper chamber.† Then his honour sent this messenger Ramajee desiring him to treat them properly. He accordingly went and treated them with respect and said, as I told you yesterday, when you go to visit [him] to-day, you had better speak to him peremptorily and arrest him. He thus spoke to the messengers of the (Foujdars) captains.

9. Next day [Ramaji] said to the messengers of the (foujdars) captains, 'Pavadapa Nayu has now given permission‡ that you should visit him: he wishes (*v* §) to give you your leave: Come.' He spoke thus to the messengers, and called them [the foujdars] in, and seated them in the stucco hall, while he himself went into the inner chamber [or seraglio] and said to Pavadapa Nayu, 'The chiefs of the host have come, please (*v.*) to come.' He [lit. *They*] too came, and an interview took place.‖ After they were seated, they said, as above mentioned, 'If you pay the tribute, well, or else you may come along with us.' On their peremptorily speaking thus, his honour said¶—At present I have no money to give you: if you have a warrant (sanad) from the Nawab, give it to me: I will place it on my head and come with you.

10. On his saying this, they angrily replied We having ourselves come is any warrant wanted? Yet never mind. We do not want you** to come with us. Pay us here the four years tribute now due and

---

(a) Page 13. "I" in the original is We."

* Because of difference of caste he could not eat with them.

† The various parts of a large Hindu house have names that do not exactly answer to any English words.

‡ Selavu, permission, often denotes command.

§ Valenu is denoted by the sign (*v.*) It is equivalent to the French il faut" or to the Latin "debet." In English it (valenu or valasinadi) is often translated *must, should, ought.* A servant says 'Tamaru selavu iyya valasinadi' that is I hope your honour will permit: literally, you must command. The negative of this is *rādu*, or *vaddu.*

‖ Here as in many other places we in English terminate a sentence, though in the original the phrase is An interview having taken place they sat down.

¶ Lit. The thing he said was.

** Lit. *Vaddu*, (for *valadu*) dont, is "il ne faut pas" in French or "Non debet" in Latin.

then rise and go.* So saying they troubled† the baron and seated him. Thus they arrested him without suffering him to go to eat or to drink. This news was heard by Nidu Mamidi Swami [confessor to the family] at the monastery in Cotta Cheruvu [the other name of Ananta Sagaram.] Thereupon he took with him all the men of that village and of Bucca Patnam and marched to Anantapuram, where he halted in his own (matham) monastery which was to the west of his lordship's palace. Then he called for his honours brother-in-law Chenna Basavappa‡ and made known [to him] all the details, saying, this is a plan laid by Ramaji to ruin the family. Then both deeply consulted what might be the best plan for extricating his honour. Then [the priest] carried Chenna Basavappa into the flower garden outside the wicket gate for the purpose, as he said, of gathering flowers for the worship of Siva [the lingam.]§

11. Then he(*) [the priest] summoned those captains of feudatories¶ who were in the village; [their names were] Singarāyani Timmaiia, and Gundla Chinnaiia, and Kanchēṭi Pāpaiia. Also (from Bucca Raya Samudram) [headmen named] Boggu Nandaiia, and Carnam Setti Peraiia, and others. He said, The hour of the fall of the family is now at hand! They have arrested his honour and kept him from meat and drink! We being so numerous it is not fit that we should merely look on while our Master is in such distress.

12. They replied, "We are mere men: what can be effected by us: both gates of the fort are in their [the Turks] hands. They look on us as old [servants] and will not suffer us to enter. When the [Turkish sardars] enemy entered the fort they merely came

---

* Meaning, you shall not stir till it is paid.

† Meaning, insulted him, harassed him.

‡ These names denote that the family were Lingavants or Vira Saivas (Jangams) the sect who wear the image of the lingam, in a box the size of a walnut, on the neck. These are considered by bramins as hereticks. The creed arose about A. D. 1160.

§ In every garden to which Hindus have access, they spoil all plants by nipping off the buds which are used as daily offerings to the gods.

(*) Page 14.

¶ *Sēruva*, a Tamil word equivalent to *Kallubadi* in Telugu; militia men, or feudal troops.

with ten [i. e. a few] men, afterwards the whole of their force [fauj] entered. If we venture to do them any wrong, they are Pathans :* as our Master has fallen into their hands, we hesitate, for there is no knowing what evil they may do him. If you will frame any scheme by which you can get our Master into the palace, afterwards we will obey your orders to the utmost of our power." Thus said they, and gave their word.

13. This (Swami†) Confessor and Chenna Basavappa "these two"‡ suggested the following plan. 'The wicket gate [or Sally-port] alone is not in their hands. Our labourers carry on the tillage§ in our own land, and bring grass for the cattle and firewood for the Household [Nagari]. You should pass on, armed, and when you come near the threshing floor in our fields, you may pack your weapons in bundles of hay: then mix with our labourers: and if ten or twenty of you daily come thus with weapons and enter with them into the house where the milch buffaloes are in the old Fort [Nagari,] meat and drink shall be provided for you from within.'

After so saying, they sent into the suburbs for a blacksmith and made him bring a file: with which they cut the bolt of the wicket gate between the outer chamber and the hall of audience: thus they made the way [sa-sūtram] clear.

14. Soon(a) there were [accordingly] two hundred men gathered, armed, in the fort. They called the former feudatories [sēruva] and said, Remain ye with your troop, in the outer suburbs: when we give you the sign, come armed to the stone gateway of the town, and stand ready. Accordingly all the men in the suburbs stood prepared. That night, about eight o'clock‖ the [Turkish] captains placed here three sepoys as a guard (over the laird,) and went away to take their supper (which was prepared) according to their own fashion ¶

---

* Pathans are a tribe of Musalmans descended from Afghanies, and viewed with detestation even by Musalmans, as hereticks and violent haughty bullies.

† Swamula varu, "His holiness"——literally the Lords; a phrase for a Guru or Confessor.

‡ It is usual after naming persons, to mention their number.

§ Here the original is carelessly worded.

(a) Page 15.

‖ Lit: after four *ghadis* of night.

¶ Ziyafat (entertainment) is probably the Arabic word meant. It is changed into వాంకిజాతిఆపోరము.

At that moment Chenna Basava who was in the palace and the [Confessor] "Cari Basava Swamulu, of Nidu-mamidi" were sitting in the square hall; called [their leaguesmen] in; and the whole troop entering stood in the open square at the chamber where they worshipped Siva. [The plotters] called four women, sensible persons, to carry in the dinner for the laird; and told them the contrivance: they accordingly conveyed the dinner inside. After the sepoys who were there arose and sat on one side [to avoid defiling them by touch, or by seeing the food,] these women gently told his honour that the way was now clear [the bolt of the wicket gate being cut] and that a body [of his lieges] had assembled. Then they unbolted the door, brought [" called"] their master in, and secured the door.

15. Meanwhile, the sepoys on guard found the mischief was done, and raised a shout: on hearing this, some (who were inside the palace) mounted on [paoti] ladders to the top of the chapel of the god Sidda Rameswar, and shot down the three sepoys, and they died. Meanwhile, the three captains, in the middle [mahl] house hearing this uproar, armed themselves, and with their men, were coming along, proposing to enter by the [hazar] great gate into the palace, and seize the Master. Meantime this Chenna Basavappa with his two hundred who were within, came through the ward-gate,* as far as the great gate: they thrust down all the (Turkish) force there, and came out and stood at the front of the outer house: an engagement took place, and many were slain. The army of the Foujdars was broken; and retreated to the stone gate of the town, and continued the fight with bows and arrows.

Then([a]) the (Servas) tributaries who were in the suburbs, came with their troops, and stood in a body at the bank of the great cemetery.† The three (Turkish "foujdars") chiefs [came] with a party, and stood in the entrance of the stone town gate and used‡ their bows and arrows to prevent any one from opposing them. Then Chenna Basavappa selected the mightiest of his men and mounted them above the marble gate: they pulled out the top stone [so as to form an embrasure] they got bags of gunpowder from the magazine, and fired it and

* Banku (Marati language) A ward of a building, misprinted *Bankam*.

([a]) Page 16.

† Pīrlu, that is the tombs of the Mahomedan *peers* or forefathers.

‡ *Vastu* should be వేస్తు *vēstu* hurling.

poured [the powder through the chink.] The three 'foujdars' could not stand this; they opened the gate and were about to come out: whereupon a feudsman on the house top fired his matchlock at one of the foujdars who fell down dead. The other two came out with their men. Chenna Basavappa with his men followed them closely and as the people* outside ran towards the (Sirdars) Turkish captains, these captains being thus between the two and fighting both, they retreated as far as the pagoda of Virūp-āxes-wara in the suburbs.

16. Meanwhile, one of the [Musulman] captains was hit in a mortal part: he fell down dead. Then as they were driven thence, when they reached the temple of Basava in the market place, the remaining captain and some of his men fell dead, and the (hata seshulu) survivors fled.

Then Pavadapa Nayu came out of the palace: he caused these three (Turkish) leaders to be buried. He took possession of their horses and furniture &c.

17. Afterwards, while a marriage was being celebrated in the house of Ramaji the ambassador from Kadapa, [Pavadapa Nayu] summoned him, told him all that was done, seized him and cast him into a dungeon† and plundered his house of all it contained.

Afterwards, Pavadapa Nayu went to wait on the god Vira Bhadra Swamy at Bucca Raya Samudram. He carried this Ramaji along with him: he secured him in the red bastion at the corner of the fort; and ordered Basavappa, a warrior who was commandant of the fort,‡ to place guards over Ramaji: then he himself proceeded to Anantapuram.

In a week after, (a) [Pavadapa Nayu] went in procession, and sent for this Ramaji. He reviled Ramaji as (swami drohi) a traitor: and as the other replied, [with revilings] he was enraged and cut out [the prisoner's] tongue. Then Ramaji thought with himself, What

* జంటికి should be జంటి.

† This resembles an anecdote in the old English ballad of Adam Bell:—

They called the porter to counsel
And wrang his neck in two &c.

‡ Rahut, or rowt, a warrior: raya, a captain.

(a) Page 17.

is the good of living maimed: [or, this infamous state,] so he tore out his tongue by the roots and died.* As soon as he was dead, as there was a waste pit there, they flung his corpse into it and cast earth and stones upon it. Then [Pavadapa Nayu] himself proceeded to Anantapuram.

This cruel murder† stared Pavadapa Nayu in the face: he ceased from meat and drink.‡

18. Before these (Musulman) officers came from the "Mayana" [a title borne by the Nabob of Kadapa] there were some Telugu tumblers who came from Duradacuntla in Rayadurgam, to the Car-feast§ in honour of Sangameswara, the god of Cuderu. They had erected their mast and were playing; among them there was a girl named Pennamma, who had but lately grown up, and who was remarkable for prettiness, grace, and elegance. [Pavadapa Nayu] saw her, and fell in love with her. He sent for her and kept her in the palace. Her father and mother came and said, we used to support ourselves by means of this girl: what orders will you give for our subsistence? Thereupon he looked out a place to the north west of Cudēru: in the Antara-Ganga land: he built a village named Muddulāpuram: and he took part of the lands of Antara ganga, and of Ooracodu, and of Chola Samudram: which lands he assigned [to Muddulāpuram.] And he granted all the revenues‖ as a living¶ to these tumblers.

19. Pavadapa Nayu, being anxious to know how he could clear himself from the guilt of the murder, consulted bramins. They replied If you will perform a pilgrimage to [the holy shrine at] Gocarna* you will be pure. Accordingly he took with him Mallappa of the

---

* Suicide in all its forms is very common among the Hindus: and this is a method often mentioned.

† Lit: *bramhatya*; though the deceased was not a bramin.

‡ Like Charles IX. after the murders of St. Bartholomew.

§ Radh' otsavam or annual feast in honour of each local god. It is a fair, and frequented by players.

‖ *Swarn-ādāyam* denotes Income, Revenue, money paid for land as rent or tribute.

¶ *Sarvamanyam*. That is, land given free from all tax.

* A holy place, lying south of the Konkan.

arsenal,* and his two wives Devamma and Girijamma: and Siddappa Nayu who was Devamma's son: he took them and set out on his journey: but while he was passing near Pedda Palem, which is twenty-six coss from Anantapuram, in the way, [the Fury† considered] that if Pavadapa Nayu reached [the shrine at] Gocarnam, she would lose her power over him. She therefore tempted him(a) and made him strangle himself and die. As soon as he died Jamdarkhana Mallappa who was along with him, covered up his Palankeen in a veil:‡ he said to the wives and child, Do not weep aloud: we are now in foreign parts: our business might (by your weeping) be greatly injured. So saying he strictly charged them: then he set out with haste for Anantasagaram (also called Cotta Cheruvu, or, Newtank.) There in the convent of the Saint Nidu mamidi, to the west of Newtank, in the year Pingala which is year 1659 of the Sālivāhana Sacam [A. D. 1737] he buried this Pavadapa Nayudu.

CHAPTER THIRD.

1. Afterwards, as Ramapa Nayu, son of Prasannapa Nayu [who was murdered by the courtezan] was not at hand, Siddappa Nayu (son of Pavadapa Nayu) was crowned, near (Cotta Cheruvu) 'Newtank' in the year Calayucti, SS. 1660 [A. D. 1738]. He thus came to the throne.§

But Siddamma the widow of Prasannapa Nayu, who was at Anantapuram, on seeing that the realm had not descended to her son, but had gone to her (maridi) husband's-younger-brother's son; fearing what evil might happen in consequence, she set out, carrying her son Ramapa Nayu; fled from Anantapuram, and went to Muddu

---

* Jam-dhar is a dagger; the repository of swords.

† Here Bramhatya, or the guilt of manslaughter is represented as a personage which we may render by a Fury or demon-goddess.

(a) Page 18.

‡ *Ghatātōp*, a Marata word for a conveyance in which a woman is concealed by veils.

§ This passage is a fair instance of inversion of style.

Mallappa Nayu of Hossūr : he being an (ancient) ally of her family. He received her very affectionately. And Siddamma died there in two months after [arrival : her son] Ramapa Nayu remained there.

2. Siddappa Nayu who was at Newtank then went to Anantapuram. He married Bhadramma; she was the younger sister of Siddamma the wife of Ballari R.* A few days after the marriage this Siddappa Nayu became a drunkard and a lewd wretch.(a) Among the married folks of the village wherever he saw pretty women, he carried them off by force and ruined them. On seeing this, the people of the two villages Anantapuram and Bucca Raya Samudram said, This lord (prabhu) is committing vile acts. So saying they quitted the villages. This news was bruited abroad through the land. The Reddis (head farmers) and clerks at Korakolla, with Ummanna the (Killadar) commandant, with the men at his station, having heard of this, considered, However long we exercise moderation with this (dora) lord, there is no end (of his misdeeds); we shall incur infamy. So saying they counselled. Ramappa the son of Prasannapa Nayu who was the late ruler† [of Anantapuram] is now in the house of Muddu Mallappa of Hossoor: he is the rightful heir to the throne. Let (v.) us bring him. So saying they went there, and stated to Muddu Mallappa and Ramapa, all that had happened here. They gave assurances to Muddu Mallapa that they would stand by him whatever might betide.‡ They took (A. P.) Ramapa along with them and arrived at Corucolla.

3. Jamdar-Khana-Mallappa§ [servant of Pavadapa Nayu,] gained the favour of Siddappa, and built a pagoda on the bank of the lake, a quarter of an hour's [walk] east of Anantapuram: this he

---

* The persons here named Ramapa and Siddamma are the namesakes of those already spoken of. Bellari Ramapa's wife was Siddamma: her younger sister was Bhadramma, wife of Siddappa son of Pavadapa Nayu; whom the demon slew.

Ramapa Nayu of Anantapur (who shall be styled (AP.) Anantapur R. was son of Prasannappa Nayu whom the dancer slew: see Chap. 2. sect. 3.) This Prasannapa N's wife was Siddamma who died at Hossoor.

(a) Page 19.

† Paṭṭapu Dora: lit: the crowned lord.

‡ Lit. for good act and bad act (or fortune) too.

§ I omit the needless words "who is now here at Anantapuram."

consecrated to saint Malleswara; he also built stairs to go down into the lake.

And Mazum-dar Ramanna (who was at Bucca Raya Samudram) dug a well which he named after himself, surrounded with trees and shrubs at the end of Santapeta ('Market-town') on the south east side of Bucca Samudram.

4. When these people, who by reason of Siddapa Nayu's outrages had left the two villages, heard of this (AP.) Ramapa's arrival at Korucolla, they repaired to him, and stated all the affair to him. They said Sir if you will honor us by coming and will garrison the two villages Anantapuram and Bucca Raya Samudram, we will abide therein. Otherwise we will depart. Accordingly (AP.) Ramapa Nayu called together the people of that neighbourhood, and coming with the people of Korucolla,(*) he garrisoned Anantapuram.

When this rebellion came to the ears of (the tyrant) Siddappa in his village, he took the weapons provided by his ancestors and some money, and left his town, to go to Tadimarri, where Pedda Tirumala Nayudu was the baron. This [Tirumala N.] said "The baron whose ancestors gave me the name of son,* the head of the family, has arrived." Accordingly he came with his troops to meet [Siddappa respectfully,] as far as the boundary at Pinnadari. He brought him in and placed him in the lodge within the fort: supplying him with all requisites:† and made enquiries regarding his health and welfare. [Siddappa] told him all that had happened here:‡ and requested him to collect some (Palegars) subsidiary captains to aid him; and to gather (his) men: he said, I request you to send forward your troops to put me again in possession of the place.

5. Pedda Tirumala Nayu replied be it so: we will aid you to the utmost of our power without fail. Thus saying he returned.

(*) Page 20

* Kumara-paddu: the title of "Son." This seems to have been like adoption; but the details are not stated. *Intitanam* literally "house-ness:" equivalent to memberhood: the being one of the family. Inti-tanam-varu may denote He who is the head of the house.

† Being of different castes they could not eat together: thus the host supplies him with undressed provisions.

‡ That is at home. The whole paragraph is obscurely worded.

Then [Pedda Tirumala Nayu] sent for his head man [prathani] A'leti Peddana, and told him the whole story regarding Siddappa N. He added, [" Take] our troops to support his lordship, and send for our allies the captains of Patti conda and Dudi conda* and from other (palems) petty posts: assemble a force, taking the command yourself: go, deliver his place again into his hands and then return to me."

Peddanna the (dalavai) commandant accordingly set out with Siddappa Nayu, at the head of all his force, and halted at the Anantapuram lake: and while they were roaming as keepers about the town (AP.) Ramappa N. [the usurper] in the fort said, The force from Tadimarri has beset the town. All the (palegars) hill chiefs have turned out on the side of this Siddappa N. The host is large. The force I have here is insufficient to check them. Thus he spoke to the militia marksmen.† He himself quitted the place. And as Murari Rayu, the son of Hindu Raya was with an army in the neighbourhood of Madaca Sarpi, [A. P. Ramapa] went with all speed to him: and said to him The task of establishing my family is yours.‡— Then he proceeded to tell all his adventures.

6. On hearing [the tale](*) Murari Rao came accordingly, with his army along with (AP.) Ramappa N. He assaulted the army of the Tadimarri family [commanded by Aleti Peddanna] and while he was plundering them, the marksmen† who were on guard in the fort said '[Surely] our own (AP.) Ramapa has come with a separate army, [to aid us].' They opened the fort-gates and came out and assaulted Aleti Peddanna's forces who were guarding the place. Then Aleti Peddanna and the other (Pā·lē-gandlu) chiefs who had come from Tādimarri seeing they were attacked on both sides, took to flight. But Murari Rao divided his troops into two bands: one marched by the Uppara-palleh route, towards the hill of Dukkala·gundam: the other

---

* Conda is a hill: *patti* is cotton in the pod: while *dudi* is cotton wool.

† Ranuva (war) gurigandlu, marksmen: apparently meaning select warriors.

‡ This is a common phrase in petitions: the writer affirming that the personage addressed is the one appointed instrument for re-establishing his family: and is responsible for its prosperity.

(*) Page 21.

marched towards Devaraconda. As they thus stood on both sides, the army led by Aleti Peddanna had no means of escape and became prisoners.

7. These prisoners came to (A.P.) Ramapa Nayu and said Sir, we are [mercenary] swordsmen. Whoever gives us employ, we serve him faithfully and perform the duty he gives us. Nothing else. The chiefs who assembled us have fled: what can be effected by us?

So (A. P.) Ramapa N. called together his head people and said These are simple folks: [lit: mere men] what have we to do with them. Take half a crown* apiece, as a poll† tax from them, and set them at liberty with their weapons. Such being his command, they accordingly paid the poll tax and went to Tādimarri.

8. Siddappa Nayu was taken prisoner (lit: was found) near Devaraconda, whence [A. P. Ramapa] brought him and secured him in the fort. Through fury he refused meat and drink and died. The public not knowing this, say that he was put to death by strangling.

9. After this Siddappa Nayu was dead, his wife Bhadramma, through heart-grief at her husband being slain, spoke to her husband's brother, (A. P.) Ramapa N. saying, It is a long time since I have seen my elder sister; if you permit me I will visit her. He therefore sent her; giving some of his people to accompany her.([a]) Bhadramma therefore set out and arrived at Bellari. She did not again return to this Ramapa of Anantapur; but she remained there.

Then the chief of Anantapuram wrote to him of Bellari,‡ requesting that "our lady Bhadramma" should be sent home again. He on reading the letter, returned an answer saying, To her ladyship can there be any difference between that place and this place? After six months we will send [her back again to you]. But the men went with her returned home to Anantapuram.

---

* Timma nayuni māda. The mada is a half pagoda: about two rupees. This particular coin is named, as it seems, from the person, Timma-nayu, who first used it. It is now unknown.

† Zuttu is the lock of hair worn by each man: pannu is a tax.

([a]) Page 22.

‡ In the original, "Anantapuram Ramapa wrote to Bellari Ramapa." The similarity of names makes it convenient to use another mode.

10. Afterwards in the year Siddharti [SS. 1661, A. D. 1739] there happened a prodigious flood in the Anantapuram tank. The waters poured over and cut the bank. As a chasm of about thirty fathoms broad was made at a place a quarter of an hour's distance from the pagoda sacred to Ganesa on the east of the village, (A. P.) Ramapa Nayu caused it to be repaired.

After six months Sācam Timma Nayudu, (who was a kinsman of the Tadimarri family,) laird of Topudurru in the Rāyadurgam country on the south west side of Hande Anantapuram* wished to obtain [the office of] keeper (Kavali) over the villages in this neighbourhood: and therefore committed outrages in the villages [on those who would not pay him black mail.]

(A. P.) Ramapa Nayu wrote to him two or three times desiring him not to perpetrate [these] vile acts: but he persisted in committing outrages.†

11. Hereupon (A. P.)Ramapa Nayu was offended. [He remembered that] in the days of his father Prasannapa Nayu, through the agency of Laççamma, elder sister of Lady Vasantamma, they had committed outrages. [See the beginning of the 2nd chapter.] And that [now] Timma Nayu is doing this mischief, in contempt‡ [of me]. Let us punish [him] and give him no ('place') quarter. He considered thus: and after some days had elapsed he got intelligence that Timma Nayu was at Topudurti: to which place therefore he made a rapid march with his troops. He stormed§ the fort and seized the town: he set Timma Nayu's little ones ‖ at liberty: but beheaded him alone. He ruined the village of Topudurru, destroyed the walls of the fort, laid the suburbs desolate, and sowed the whole ruins with oil seed. Then he again returned to Anantapuram.

---

* This sentence exemplifies the countermarch that happens in translating from the southern languages into English.

† Chillara caryamulu: literally, mean or petty acts.

‡ Tat-sādhanamuga—lit. by this means: the other manuscript says tātsāramga, negligently: that is, "in contempt of me."

§ Laggalu, are ladders used in storming a fort.

‖ Lit. with small and little.

12. After two years, (a) this (A. P.) Ramappa N. wished to recapture his own village Kanumukkula, which was [formerly] seized by Koneti Rao of Raidurgam. He marched with his bands from Buccapatnam, bringing scaling ladders: he set them up against the fort of Kanumukkula; but before [the swordsmen] could mount up, the people in that town with the leader Erra* Nagi Reddi were aroused; they threw down the ladders and drove the baron of Anantapuram to flight. Then [Erra Nagi Reddi] wrote a letter to [his lord] Koneti Rao, of Raya Durgam; who on reading it was displeased. He marched with his troops to Buccapatnam; and as the lake was not full he halted there: he besieged the town and set (mōrjā†) batteries against it; and as he made it a close‡ siege, one Virappa, who was commandant and superintendent of the place, wrote and sent a letter to his lord (A. P.) Ramappa stating that "the village is closely besieged, and there is no relief [to be hoped]: if you will within four or five days bring a force and raise the siege, well: otherwise the village will fall into their hands."

13. When this reached Ramapa he read it, and immediately set ready the troops and the horse that were here: and he wrote a letter to Sānē Narasimha Nayu, at Peddapalem, stating that "Buccapatnam is now besieged; please (v.) to come and assist in raising the siege." This letter he gave to the hand of Narayanappa the (desai) head man, saying "set out from hence, deliver this letter, and summon Narasimha Nayu with all speed; come to the Puttu Parru border, and then send me word."—So saying he sent him. Then this (A. P) Ramapa Nayu set out with his troopers. They deviated from the road, and went into the Tadimarri country: they then rapidly marched by the Mallemgonda route, and entered Buccapatnam by the gate at the chapel of Saint Someswara.

(a) Page 23.

* Many family names have a particular import. Erra means Red, or fair: not black.

† Morja (Persian mōrcheh) is explained a battery: but a mound or bank might be the best interpretation. See 2 Sam. xx. 15. Ezek. xvii. 17. Or, approaches; See Johnson's quotation from Dryden.

‡ Cheru: the *root in U* of cheruta, to approach.

14. The next day Naraianappa who had gone to Pedda Palem brought Sāneh Narasimha Nayu's troops, came, according to orders, and reaching the Puttu Parti boundaries, sent tidings of this to his master (A. P.) Ramapa N. in the fort.(a) [He sent back a message saying] you should march with your troops on the bank, and pass before the pagoda of Sainte Chaudeswari.* Then he sounded the kettle drums (Nagara, Naqārah,) in the fort, and [coming] with those captains whom he relied on as trustworthy, he caused the fort gate to be opened and came out: he attacked the approaches, and fought. While he was so engaged, the troops from Peddapalem who had come from (Santa topu) Market-grove, entered the Fair-town-gate with drums and trumpets.

15. Thus the leaders, with the troops engaged in the approaches within the suburbs, being between the two hosts fell into [Ramapa's] hands. He wished to seize [Coneti Rao of Raya Durgam]. Then, as with both troops [A. P. Ramapa] was going to the place where [Coneti Rao] now was, Coneti Rao heard of this affair from the survivors. He saw that his own troops were flying in confusion, with their hair loose: he said, If I halt here I have no chance. He quitted his tents and made a flying march to Kanumuccala in his own country: there he remained ten days: and then went to (his home at) Raidurgam.

When [A. P.] Ramapa Nayu heard these tidings, he in four days marched to [Hande] Anantapuram.

16. Afterwards Coneti Rao of Raidurgam, grieved to the heart at his defeat, (again) summoned all his troops, and marched with all his force and besieged the village, named Muctāpuram, six coss (about 13 miles) from Anantapuram. After five or six days, Condi Reddi† and the clerks and all the people in this Muctāpuram, wrote a letter to Ra-

---

(a) Page 24.

* The temples of the various gods are to this day the marks whereby the various quarters are known in the town of Madras. Our Lady Chaudeswari is the same as Sainte Durga or mother Kali the amiable goddess after whom Calcutta is named. The Greeks called her Cotytto the good goddess. See Juvenal's sixth Satire.

† The Reddis or petty barons, ruled the Telugu country from A. D. 1320 until 1498. At present this title is borne by head-farmers, or petty chiefs.

mapa Nayu of Anantapuram saying: "Our village is closely besieged, there is no prospect of escape: what advice do you give us?" On receiving and reading the letter he instantly in broad daylight sounded drums: and marched with all the men whom he had at hand: he halted in the neighbourhood of Marūru: and next day, at noon, he [again] sounded the drums, and marched and fell upon the besiegers. All the people in the fort being delighted that their Master had come and attacked [the enemy], came out also and assaulted the foe. And as the people(*) on both sides attacked [Coneti Rao's troops] they fled leaving even their baggage, and ran away home to Kanagānapalle. Then A. P. Ramapa Nayu stayed in this village until Coneti Rao reached Rayadurgam. After that he went [home] with his troops and arrived at Anantapuram.

17. Afterwards, as in a few days there was abundant rain, the tanks of the three upper villages (viz.) Rāmagiri, Baddalāpuram, and Cōnāpuram had burst, and the flood descended. And as the two sluices of the tank did not suffice [to let the stream pass] the bank was breached to the extent of thirty fathoms at a quarter of an hour's distance on the south east of Anantapuram.* [But] Two or three months after, Ramapa N. [laird of Anantapuram] repaired the tank.

18. While Ramapa N.† [of Anantapuram] was thus continuing his rule,‡ Lady Bhadramma, (widow of Siddappa N. son of Pavadapa N.) who had formerly gone from hence to Bellari [See section 9 above] spoke to her elder sister Siddamma, wife of Ramapa (laird of Bellari): and related the particulars of the death of her husband Siddappa Nayu [laird of Anantapuram, the drunkard: younger brother to Ramapa Laird of Anantapur.] And through her [Siddama] she [Bhadramma] communicated the tale [of the murder; see section 8th,] to her brother-in-law [that is, to the laird of Bellari.] She said: While so noble a chief as you is my (bāva) brother-in-law,

---

(*) Page 25.

* A quarter of an hour means about two hundred yards.

† Wherever the author uses I' (or EE, meaning *this*, as Ī Ramappa, he means Anantapur: and A' ("that," or "the other") denotes Bellari.

‡ The following sentence, clear enough to a native, is intricate to an Englishman.

ought I to be in this plight? If, in revenge for slaying my husband, you will slay [" bava"] my husband's elder brother, Ramapa N. laird of Anantapuram, it will be a content to my mind.

As she and her elder sister urged him with such words night and day, for a long time, he laid up these words in his heart, and planned how he might soonest accomplish the work.

His (bava maridi) brother-in-law named Zaggula Mallappa had the (dalavai-tanam) office of commandant under Ramapa laird of *Anantapur*. Then he (Ramapa of *Bellari)* sent him [several] treacherous letters secretly.

19. Thereupon this Zaggula Mallapa considered [and wrote in reply to him saying.] If you suddenly set out from thence [and attack my lord] it will not be practicable for you to master this family. You should *(v)* manage it by (Mitra-bhedam) cunning. That is:— [you should have letters written to (A. R.) my master saying:(ᵃ)] " As I have no male offspring,(ᵃ) if you will give me a son to rear, both houses will be yours:" if you write thus [Z] and send from thence persons of honour who may be trusted; [I] will get the letters delivered here, and get [your messengers,] young and old, introduced, and [I] will speak so that he may bestow one of his sons on you. Thus [I] can induce the belief that, that family and this family are in reality one: then I will get him to write you letters of reply and will send them. Afterwards confidence will be restored between you. Thus he wrote in reply.

When Ramapa, laird of Bellari, read these letters, he considered, It is all just as it should be: then according to his (baomaridi) brother-in-law Zaggula Mallappa's advice he wrote letters which he gave into the hands of Zanivāram Rama Chandra Nayac; and Curugodu Surappa, and Zunjā Bhai the Turaca [i. e. Musulman] whom he caused to set out, and sent them with vests, and vessels, as marks of homage.

20. They accordingly set out and went* to Anantapuram where they spoke with this Zaggula Mallappa; he placed them

---

(ᵃ) Page 26.

* Literally *came*: one of the many instances that *go* and *come* are often used one instead of the other.

outside [the fort] while he went in, to the presence of Ramapa, laird of Anantapuram and said, Honorable persons have come bearing letters from Ramapa laird of Bellari; and have halted outside [your citadel.] You should call them in, grant them an interview, and receive and read their letters, and send them on their way. The laird replied, "For many days past no letters have passed between them and us! Yet, what matters it? When honourable persons come, let us admit them." On his saying so, this Zaggula Mallappa came to the outside [of the castle] and said to the visitors. "If [my lord] asks what did [your lord] say by word of mouth? you must reply saying Our master has addressed a letter to you expressing his wish to have one of your sons." Then he carried them in [to the castle] and introduced them to the laird of Anantapur, who asked [them] "What is the news?" They replied before his honour according to what he [Mallappa] had instructed them to say, and delivered the letters to his hand. He took them, broke the envelopes, and read them. According as they had stated(a) [the letters] were written requesting a son [for the purpose of adoption]. He was well-pleased: and considered that this would put both families into his hands. So he gave these honourable persons [a room for] lodging, and sent, out of his granary, rice, grain, and other eatables of every kind, and directed this Zaggula Mallappa to tend them night and day: so he sent them to their apartments.

21. Afterwards this laird of Anantapuram called this Zaggula Mallappa who was with him, and some of his older women,* and read to them the letters which had come to him from Bellari, and said "They have written saying, If you will bestow a boy [on us] that we may rear him, this our family [shall become] yours; now if we consider the state of things it is the fact that they have [i. e. *he has*] no male offspring: and they have written for a boy. It seems to me [lit. to my mind] that it will be well to give them a boy; and thus get their house into our power. Now what advice do you [ladies] give about this?" Those noble ladies* considered in their hearts, "It is in his honour's heart to bestow a boy on them,

(a) Page 27.

* Pedda manushulu. Literally, Great personages, Dames.

so as to establish a family: it is therefore not fit to give a [contradictory] reply." So they said: "All matters (artham) are thoroughly known to my lord; and we too think it is best that the two families should be (eca grîvam) united."

22. Thereupon, next day this Ramappa Nayu of Anantapuram, in the morning, sent for the honourable men who had come from Bellary and said "My elder brother [this is the same as His lordship, his honour] has been so gracious to us, as to state that having no heir, he desires me to send him a son: about this what hesitation is there?" So saying, he declared by word of mouth in their presence, "I have given my eldest son, Sidda Ramappa Nayu aged* twelve years, to Ramapa, laird of Bellari and added a letter shall be written concerning this to [my] elder brother: and whatever he writes back we will act accordingly."

The visitors, small and great were much pleased(a) at this. Then they wrote [a letter] saying They have granted us Sidda Ramapa Nayu [as an heir] for our family: with all the particulars. When the laird of Bellari read this letter, he called his wife Siddamma, and (maradalu) his wife's younger sister [the widow] Bhadramma, to whom he stated all that had passed. [The ladies said] "If you will, by making any plan, accomplish our wishes it will please us much." So they [the ladies] retired into the (antahpuram) inner palace.

23. The next day the laird of Bellari [wrote a letter to small and great† to this effect‡] "My [dear] younger brother [a mere phrase of courtesy] has done according to my wishes. You are now to present to the various personages the vests of honour which I entrusted to you, in proportion to their dignity, and gratify them: you are to bring the lad along with you according to my "younger brother's" promise in a fortunate [astrological] hour; you must

---

* Some have believed that in old days the Hindus obeyed the laws of Menu: wherein the adoption of an *eldest* son is forbidden: and the child adopted must be less than five years old. Here both rules are broken. But these southern highlanders cared little for law.

(a) Page 28.

† Pinna peddalu, great and small: the public, every body.

‡ These words come in at *Z*.

halt at the pagoda of Saint Basava at the Sonahalli river, and send me word : whereupon I will come out and bring him [with honour] into town. [*Z.*]

They stated the whole matter in writing to the Anantapuram laird, who was well pleased.

24. These messengers laid before the laird of Anantapur the vests and vessels which they had brought : and caused all [the personages] to be gratified proportionably to their rank. Then he delivered his eldest son Sidda Ramapa, into their charge, saying " This is a child: [tell his honour my elder brother[a]] whether he understands [wisdom] or knows it not, to tend and guard him is THEIR [that is, his honour your master's] province [Z]." He gave some people and some horse to accompany them ; and packed up some *vessels* and vests of honour to be delivered to the personages " there."

He said, " Lay these at the feet of my elder brother, requesting that he will distribute them to whosoever is to receive them according to each person's rank." Then he bestowed some vests and other things on the messengers, and they with their troops set forth. They halted at the stream of Sonahalli which is within half a coss of Bellari, and sent word [to their master.]

25. Then([a]) the laird of Bellari came forth with his army of all descriptions* and on seeing the lad, Sidda Ramappa, he [the boy] bowed down at his feet : [he] raised [him] embraced [him] mounted [him] on [his own] elephant, carried him [with all pomp] into the town, and seated him on the throne : [he] summoned all [his] host and made them adore him (the son); and conducted him into the (nagari) palace where [he] caused [him] to adore the Dame† and was very loving to him.

To all the guards and marksmen who had gone hence [from Anantapur] with the lad, he distributed suitable food and vestments ; he lodged them in another locality. He thus entertained

---

([a]) Page 29.

* A respectable phrase for a party of perhaps 400 spears and twenty matchlocks.

† Ammagaru : an honorific phrase for a mother.

the party for four days; and he wrote a long letter to the laird of Anantapuram, and directed that there should be continual letters stating to each family whatever happened in the other: then he dismissed them. The troop, horse and foot, arrived at Anantapuram and delivered these letters: which the laird of that place perused with much gratification.

After four days had passed in this manner, by means of letters the two families became (sasutram) firmly connected. On questioning persons who came from thence, he was delighted at hearing that the young gentleman was most lovingly fostered.

CHAPTER FOURTH.

1. After a year had passed in this manner [the laird of Bellary wrote a letter saying z] to him of Anantapuram. "The little lord is very anxious to see you [again :] your lordship has never visited us here: as the two houses are now united into one, it is needless for you to retain in your mind the doubts of former days. Please to consider it. By all means set out on the journey: come with all your troops of all kinds: and see us and the little lord with your eyes,(a) and stay here four [meaning, a few] days and then return: my heart will then be at ease. [Z*]

The laird of Anantapur after reading this letter called for his (samayājica) managers and Jaggulamallappa the commandant: he said to them, "I am going to Bellary to have an interview with his honour [my] elder brother, and I shall come [home] in a week. Be ye therefore cautious regarding the fort, the guards, the reliefs, and so forth.

So saying, he set out with all his force, and halting at the stream of Sonahalli he sent word [into the fort of Bellary.] And on hearing of this the laird of Bellary came forth with all his troops of all arms† and

---

(a) Page 30.

* Here come in the first words of this paragraph placed between brackets.

† Chaturanga: which here means a few matchlocks, bows and arrows, spears and clubs.

paid his respects: then he took [his guest] with him and invited him saying, Let us go into the palace. Then the laird of Anantapur replied saying It is the same as my coming to the palace.* Then he pitched his tents on the plain near the sally port of the fort, which leads towards the Nagal cheru (Snake Tank,) road, and halted with his infantry and cavalry. The dinner was sent him from within the Bellari palace.†

2. After four days had thus passed, the laird of Bellari fancied that the laird of Anantapur entertained some suspicions in his heart; so he sent his troops and horse out of the fort [of Bellari,] and called the Anantapur troops into the fort: and delivered the keys and seals into his guest's hands. This caused much reliance: and he dwelt at ease for four days.

At that time, the laird of Bellary secretly called his three [captains,] named Ramachandra N. of Zanivāram, and Surappa of Curugōdu, and Zunza bhai the Turk. He counselled with them saying Let us play a trick here to this Anantapur Ramapa. They replied "If [we] wrong him here, will the matter end with him alone? as his sons and sons-in-law are in great numbers there [at Anantapur] they can draw the family to that side as usual and certainly (literally, when it dawns) they will wage war with us. They have a large family, [or many kinsfolk;] while we are (vantari gandlam) a small people. Let us not make any plot here. Let us treat these our guests with honour, and homage, and, when they go, send them away most kindly:(*) thus shall they assuredly invite you home to their city: then you will answer that you will come after a short time: you will bestow every honour upon them, and let them believe that the place is theirs: this will, in future, be a great help‡ to our plot." Thus they spoke and he consented.

3. After ten days had passed in this manner, the laird of Anantapuram said to him of Bellari, It is ten days since we came here:

---

* A courteous refusal.

† In the original this looks like a contradiction. By omitting the word *majjanam* it may become clearer. It seems to mean that he went into the fort to dine and to bathe.

(*) Page 31.

‡ Sādhacam, means, way, instrument.

if you will permit us we will return home. I pray that you also will favour us by coming* with all your army, and see with your eyes all [your] kinsfolk there, young and old, and remain there four days, and then return. As he earnestly invited them, [the laird of Bellari replied saying] what matter though we come: [that is, we make no objection:] please to go (padandi) home. I will put the fort in safe hands, and after four days I will come to you.

So saying he presented vests and vessels and other gifts to the laird of Anantapur with his managers, so as to gratify them: then he dismissed them. So they returned to their home at Anantapuram.

4. Thus the laird of Bellary remained there: and therefore within three or four days the laird of Anantapuram wrote him letters of invitation, praying him to come speedily. When he of Bellary read these letters he caused replies to be written promising that he would come. These he sent beforehand and then set out with his troops: he halted on the west side of the village Rāçāna palleh, on the bank of the Tadacaleru [that is, the river "Wisp"] and sent word to Anantapuram. On hearing the news, the laird of Anantapuram set out with his sons, accompanied by his troops of all arms, and proceeded towards the rock of Rāçāna palleh; where the laird of Bellari came to meet him from the Tadacaleru. They had an interview: they embraced each other and he of Bellary put a gilt† necklace on the neck of his friend: then they with their troops proceeded to Anantapuram, and were about to enter the fort: but he of Bellari([a]) observed "I have brought both horse and foot, a large force, with me: there will be no room for them in the fort. By your leave we will halt at the Great Mosque-Bank." [See Chap. 2. 15.] But his host replied "why do you condescend to say so?" Thereupon he removed all his guards and troops out of the fort, and sent them into the suburbs; and instead, he brought the Bellary troops into the fort and placed them on guard, and lodged his lordship in the palace. That night he supplied supper and baths and all

---

* Observe the aorist phrase *vatturu gani* denoting I hope you will come. In Latin *Veniatis.* And *Padandi,* please to go; *Eatis.*

† This seems an error: as no Hindu will use gilded ornaments.

([a]) Page 32.

else requisite in the palace, and sent every man that came, his food according to his caste.

5. Afterwards the marksmen and Managers of Anantapuram, addressed their chief, saying; "Is all this intimacy consistent with safety? To remove our sentinels and substitute theirs is not fitting. Let our own guards stand." But the laird of Anantapur was angry at their words and said, "Do not tell me such cock and a bull stories.* I alone know what ground I have for confidence. You must all go down into the suburbs."

Then replied Naranappa the (desai) headman, to his lord (dhanī;) "Listen to my request. At the hour of your birth the God Budha (Woden) was the malevolent star: and he is to-morrow in the ascendant: his day too, [Wednesday,] is to-morrow: and there is no probability that we shall to-morrow be able to see your honour: all is ended† between you and me." Such was his peremptory declaration: he took leave and came out: and every man went home.

6. Afterwards the laird of Bellari sent word by Munē Virabhadra, to his honour [of Anantapuram] saying, "To-morrow if your lordship pleases I wish to ride to Buccapatnam," "Very well: let us go accordingly" replied he of Anantapuram.

It was the custom with the laird of Anantapuram to be shaved‡ every Wednesday: accordingly he sent for Peda Timmadu the barber, and said; To-morrow I am going on an excursion; and must be shaven by sunrise: therefore sleep here. Then he ordered that this man should be given his dinner in the palace: and accordingly the man lay there.

7. Then the laird of Ballary called Jaggula Mallappa, and Munē Vira Bhadrappa, and Rama Chandra N. of Zanivaram, and Surapa of Curugōdu, and Zunzā Bhai the Musulman, and others.(a) He seated them and took counsel. He observed that "At the hour when it is about to dawn§ while shaving, no people are [likely to be] in attendance; that is the time to smite and ruin him." He

* Literally Tales of puddings boiled in milk.

† Runam tirinadi—"The debt is paid: that is, I have no further obligation."

‡ *A'yushcarmam* "the dues of age" a common phrase for shaving.

(a) Page 33.

§ Tellavara; from *Tella* white, and *pārula* to flow: "when the light spread."

therefore picked out fitting men for the purpose, and kept them in readiness with their weapons. Presently it drew towards dawn, and the laird of Anantapuram called the barber: he sat down and was being shaved.

Those villains told the laird of Bellari, 'This is the proper moment.' So he sent some trustworthy swordsmen, named Nīladu, and Cōdē* Nīladu, and Guruvadu, with others. He armed them with Codugu-swords† and other weapons, and sent them in. They entered and struck off the head of the laird of Anantapuram. The barber Peda Timmadu fled out backwards, by the sally port, went into the suburbs, and told the news.

8. Then all the people in the suburbs collected in a body at the Cattulūr‡ gate, and stood armed. The wives and sons, and other people of Anantapuram Ramapa Nayu, who were in the palace, set up cries and shrieks; and when this Niladu and others came and told their master, Ramapa of Bellari, that they had cut off the laird's head, he sent guards to stop the people in the palace from howling. When the laird of Bellari heard that the towns folk had assembled, armed, and ready for combat, he ordered his men to fasten the [murdered] laird's head on a pole, and to exhibit it at the Tiger's head§ [gate.] All beheld the head and cried Treason! they came back, and stood in a crowd at the Herd-meadow.

As soon as this news was told to the laird of Bellari, he called for Zaggula Mallappa and told him to pacify the multitude: and to send them all to their homes. This man came and said, Whatever has happened has been done by the will of God.‖ "Thus he pacified them, and reassured the troops and sent them away.

---

* Code means younger. It is generally used of cattle.

† That is bill hooks: such as are used in Coorg.

‡ Cattul-ūr, the name of a village, means "Swords" the name of a well known battle field, in England.

§ Huli, Kannadi word for a tiger.

‖ This is an instance of a ruling principle of the Hindus: attributing every good and every evil act, to predestination: this is strongly insisted on in the Introduction to the Hitopadesa. This principle destroys all moral responsibility, and we sometimes find the Hindus (like Job's wife) cursing God for misfortunes.

Thus was Ramapa Nayadu of Anantapuram slain: on Wednesday the 9th of the wane in the month Jyestha, year Angirasa; 1674 of the Salivahana Era. [6th of June, A. D. 1752] at two (gharis) Indian hours after dawn.

9. Afterwards([a]) this Ramapa, laird of Bellari caused the [Anantapuram] citadel to be guarded vigilantly, and placing in it a commandant with a small garrison, he sent his men out, over the country. Excepting the towns of Rāptād, Buccapatnam, and Cotta-cheruvu, all the lands fell into his hands, and he placed garrisons throughout. To govern these lands he called Ramachandra the captain,* and Jaggula Mallappa the commandant, and others: he said to them "Go ye, and speak to the head-farmers, the clerks, the managers, the merchants and shopkeepers, the swordsmen and warriors and others: and say, Wherever there was enmity against us we have done it away: [Go and tell them] that all of them should continue their occupations, every man in his own sphere; let every man be as usual. Speak and reassure and pacify them thus and return to me." So saying Ramapa sent them into the town. Accordingly they went and comforted the folks. When the (Reddis, Curnums) reeves, clerks and others heard these words, they met and consulted among themselves, and said "If we take service with this (durmarg) wretch, we shall lose our honour. He deluded our old lord and slew him. We cannot dwell here." Such was their reply to Zaggula Mallappa and the rest. But he replied "As it is our (Dhani) Chief's command, you who please, dwell here: you who are displeased depart."

Being too distrustful to remain, the whole people of Anantapuram and Bucca Raya Samudram instantly emigrated into the Tadimarri country.

10. Afterwards, the Bellari Chieftain Ramapa took the Anantapuram chief's son Siddappa [whom he had pretended to adopt] and [the same Anantapuram chieftain's] son-in-law Basavappa (of the Karihuli family). He linked them together, by chains fastened on

---

([a]) Page 34.

* The following passage contains appellations which have no *precise* equivalent in English.

their legs; and sent them off with a guard, whom he desired to secure them [in the prison] on the hill at Bellary: he kept the [widowed] wives, and female children here [in Anantapuram] in the palace: but all the sons and other males he knocked on the head.

He seized all the treasury, the weapons, provisions for war, and other wealth, and dispatched it to Bellary. He appointed the captain Ramachandra, and Surapa of Curugōdu, and Mallappa of the Zaggula family and Zunza Bhai the Turk,(a) and others, as plenipotentiaries here [in Anantapuram]. He even took the [idol of] saint Siddha Rameswara [out of the chapel there] and marched with his troops and arrived at Bellary.

11. Four months after these occurrences, this [luckless] Sidda Ramapa Nayu, who was imprisoned on the hill at Bellary, and [his fellow bondsman] Cari huli Basavapa, being both linked together with one fetter on one foot [of each], Almighty God's (Sri Devu) mercy was shewn to Basavapa: and he formed a scheme: one day, at night they very humbly besought the jailors who were on the perpetual guard, saying, This day after it dawns, they will take our lives: bestow ye our lives (prāna dānam) on us, and deliver (nirvāhacam) our family. We will light a lamp* and remember you night and day with gratitude.

Then by the grace of God the jailors' hearts being moved, and pity arising, they severed the shackle from off [his] leg: and Basavappa [as a faithful liegeman] laid [his liege lord] Siddappa [whose leg was shackled] on his shoulders, and proceeded; the guards being his guides; they passed by the secret [literally *thief*-path] way, and came out into the plain of the Nagala-Tank. Then the guards pointing, said to his honour Basavappa,† "This is the Hirēhālu road: it is about to dawn: depart with speed." So the [guards] returned into the town, taking their own little ones, and quitted the village, and departed by another way.

(a) Page 35.

* Alluding to the custom of the Musulmans, borrowed from that of the Jews: alluded to in such passages as "the light of the wicked shall be put out."

† "Basavappa Gāru" that is, "His honour Basavappa."

12. After it dawned, as [the fugitives] Basavappa and his honour Siddaramappa, having been in prison without (anna-saralam) proper food, they were unable to walk [further.] So, when they entered the field which was before the hamlet Haradalu, under the village Hirē-hal, being faint and very hungry, Siddappa said to Basavappa; If our enemies come and catch us, let them: [there's an end of all:] I am hungry. So saying, he sat down under a tree: which was within [two parugus, i. e. coss] four miles of Hirēhāl. Hereupon Basavapa Nayu thought in his heart "Behold! Though we have once escaped, the hour is come for us to fall again into their hands."

But by the mercy of God, there came an honest man, of the Balija caste, out of this Hire-hāl: he was a Reddi (burgher): he cultivated a rye-field* and had reaped it: and stacked [the grain]. He now came for the purpose of getting the crop trodden out, and made into grain: he brought his cattle and men, and their breakfast in vessels, and water: as he was([a]) passing along he saw the two men sitting under a tree with fetters on their legs.† He asked who are you, and whence come you? Then Basavappa related all their adventures to the burgher, and said, "If you will in this (evil) hour supply us with bread and water, and conceal us from the view of all persons, you will have the virtue of having granted us our lives." By the grace of God he felt compassion for them, and comforted them saying "Be not afraid." He thus reassured them; and seating Sidda Ramapa on his own bullock,‡ and taking Basavappa along with him, brought them into his field-threshing-floor: there he at once served up to them the breakfast that he there had, and hid them among the heaps of rye.

13. Afterwards, a marksman, who had charge of the guard on the hill at Bellari, came, and looking into the guard room, he saw that

---

* Corralu, a certain grain.

([a]) Page 36.

† Probably the shackle remained on the master's leg alone, and he was therefore borne by Basavappa.

‡ It is worthy of remark, that however miserable his situation, the feudal chief is always reverenced by the Hindu, as well as by the Scotch Highlander and the Arab.

their own men the guards who were on duty, and the captives in irons, Siddaramappa and Basavapa were not there. He searched about the hill for an hour, and made up his mind that they had fled: so he came down [the mountain,] and told the fact to Ramapa the chieftain of Bellari. He was in a great rage; he summoned his men and horse and sent them out in all directions for six miles, ordering that wherever the [fugitives] should be found they should be chastised and brought back.

14. Then the [marks]—men and riders searched on all sides, and seeing a multitude near that field, four riders came to take notice: but were answered by the Reddi and others, thus: When we came out of town there were two men-persons going along the Kudutani road, a long way off, and we saw them. But nobody has since come along this road. On hearing these words, they proceeded along the Kudutani road, and after looking around on all sides, the whole body, horse and foot, went back and said to Ramapa Nayu "They have no where appeared." Thereupon he reflected thus: "Those who fell into my hands have disappeared: they [must] have had divine assistance: it is uncertain what may happen in future." Such were his reflections.

15. Afterwards(*) the head man (Reddi) of Hirehāl, after evening fell, took Basavapa and Sidda Ramapa Nayu out of the rye-straw, and carried them to his own house: he got [them] bathed, and caused whatever food there was in the house to be given them: he sent for an ironsmith and made him take the fetter off the leg of Basavappa. Then he gathered some people of his village: he had them mounted on two bullocks, and with a crowd [of attendants] he conveyed them to Hirehāl; where he told all the matter to Sivappa the Ameen [or local magistrate] who carried on the business of the town, under [the Marata chief] Murari Rao. Committing the two [hapless wretches] to him, he himself took leave and went home to his village.

(*) Page 37.

CHAPTER FIFTH.

1. Afterwards this Sivappa [who managed the village of Hirēhālu,] observing the arrival of these two, asked them "Who are you? what is your father's name?" [Sidda Ramaya replied *] I am the son of Ramapa Nayu, of Anantapur: my name is Sidda Ramapa: this man is my (bava maridi) brother-in-law; his name is Basavappa: such is our history. [z]

Now as he [the Manager] had heard from many people the whole history of these [two] he felt much (tapatrayam) compassion. [He replied saying z] The afflictions you have hitherto suffered have now passed by: by the grace of God you shall hereafter enjoy better days: be not afflicted: [z] so saying he consoled them. He added "How do you dine? I will send eatables for you to a Balije house."*

They replied "We came here just after having taken a meal at the house of the Gaudu [headfarmer] of that village: we are not hungry." Thereupon his honour Sivappa called the servants who made his bed, and ordered them saying, Prepare beds for both [the refugees] in the porch before the house;† then, after they have lain down, come to me. He also directed the people who lay in the hall, saying, Be ye watchful over these [strangers]. He gave the tambulam‡ [a solemn sign of security] to them, and said, Go and sleep at your ease. (a) Then he himself went to bed.

2. Accordingly this Sidda Ramapa and Basavappa lay down to sleep in the gate. Next day his honour Sivappa called for them and appointed the house of a Balje-caste man in the fort, [for them to lodge in]: he also gave them a (dalayit) page of his own, to attend them: and ordered his shopkeeper to give the page who might come from them, whatever (veççam) daily supplies were required, and to set it down in his own account. He then sent for a barber, and

---

* Because these two were of the Balije caste.

† Hazaram: the chamber or open hall at a town gate or palace gate; the lodge.

‡ The Tambulam, or paun leaf is among the Hindus equivalent to a glass of wine after dinner among Europeans: it is also given in solemn asseverations or promises.

(a) Page 38.

caused them to be shaved* clean, and let them perform the purificatory [or ceremonial] bathe; he also gave them suitable vestments and dishes and thus arranged every thing.

As his (dhani) prince, Murari Rao† was at this time (A. D. 1752) warring in the Chirata-nā-pali (Trichinopoly) country, he wrote the particulars of all these occurrences and sent them [to Murari Rao] adding "I shall act according to the orders I may receive from you." On reading his letter Murari Rao observed:—"The Handē family is very ancient, [lit: of many days:] Providence (daivam) should‡ not have brought such affliction on them: thus spoke he, feeling much commiseration (tāpa trayam) for their hard hap. He said: "I (lit: We) have written and sent a letter to Kuditini Zantangi Raya too: whatever aid these young gentlemen ask you to grant, he and thou must offer to the utmost in your power without fail: and whatever you find impracticable (sādhyam cānidi) you must make known to me by letter: and I will take every care for them." Such was the reply which he wrote to Sivappa.

3. A month passed in this manner: when, one day Basavappa went to Sivappa the (āmīn) magistrate, and said If we thus sit still, how can our business be settled? If you will keep [his honour] Siddha Ramapa N. here, and send me with suitable aid, I will accomplish the deed in your name, and bring you celebrity. Such was the request made by Basavapa.

Sivappa consented: he kept the young baron [Sidda Ramapa] with him, and sent Basavapa [with a fitting force;] giving him a horse, proper weapons, and clothes, and some money,(*) and men. He set out and marched to the Chitra callu, and Pedda palem families, and raised some allies; then he arrived at Rāptād, a village which had not fallen into the hands of the laird of Bellari.

---

* Ayushcarmam: see note on page 36.

† The Marata chieftain who ruled Golconda and was a conqueror in Southern India: the first volume of Orme's History gives an ample narrative of his victories.

‡ Terādu (from teççuta to bring, and vaççuta to come:) rādu is the negative of valasinadi. In Latin it might be rendered Deos ita agere nefas: it is dreadful that the Deity should thus deal with them.

(*) Page 39.

4. The late laird of Anantapuram had formerly bestowed the (kumara pattam,) title of "*Son*" on a marksman at Rāptād named Mekala Chinnaiia [that is Chinnaiia of the goats]: by reason of this honour he came to receive Basavapa Nayu, and fell at his feet, and then conducted him in; saying—Your making your escape, by the grace of God (swamidaya) is a great means [of victory.] Then Mecala Chinnaiia first wrote letters in his own name to the lairds* of Buccapatnam, Cotta cheruvu, Maruru, Muctapuram and other places; they on reading [the letters] said "Our old masters have come again." They were much pleased and came with their followers to offer gifts: they came to Basavapa Nayudu.

There was formerly a merchant at Anantapuram, named Anantaiia of the Baiianna family, who lodged at a village named Chiia durgam in the Tādimarri country. Mecala Chinnaiia wrote letters to him: on receiving them he was much gratified: he instantly set out and went to Rāptād where he visited his honour Basavappa. Then his honour narrated to him all his lucky and luckless adventures from the beginning. Then [the merchant] said, "You have come here through many afflictions: hereafter you have no occasion to grieve for any thing: as far as is in my power I will aid you with money: whatever steps you think proper to take regarding politicks, I hope you will take them." So saying he took leave of his honour Basavappa. Then Anantaiia came into the Rāptād suburbs, and supped and lay down to sleep.

5. The next day Basavappa, reflecting on what this Anantaiia had said, called for Mecala Chinnaiia who was at Raptadu, and said to him, "Baiianna-gari-Anantaiia the (comati) merchant will provide batta for the troops. You are to receive the benevolences which are brought by [our friends] who have assembled from Buccapatnam, Cotta Cheruvu, Marūr,(a) Muctāpuram and Gondi-Reddi's hamlet and other places; and give bread to such as have brought forces. Then assemble the army."

So saying [Basavanna] gave the assembled rusticks and the army into [Chinnaiia's] hands: while he himself went to Vemula and

* Desasthulu: natives, inhabitants.

(a) Page 40.

visited Comāra Nayu. Then [Basavappa] said "I shall come with some troops in ten days, and I wish you to remain on your guard [there] with your troops at Rāptād." Thus saying he sent him to Rāptād. Then [Basavappa] set out and went to Great Vemula where he waited on Peda Comāra Nayu who received him with much honour and listened to all his good and bad adventures, feeling (tapatraya) compassion for him. He said "As far as lies in my power I will help you without any slackness. Be not afflicted." So saying he encouraged [Basavappa] and kept him there ten days: granting him clothes, and other articles [of honour,] and took care that the proper supplies were furnished to him. Then giving some troops under the command of Yerra Golla Ramapa* he gave leave [to his guest Basavappa] and thus set him forward on his journey.

6. Afterwards Basavapa, accompanied by these troops, went through Buccapatnam, to Banda-mīdi-palleh,† and Kūdēru, and Koracolla, and other places, and (upagramamulu) the petty hamlets. In them he placed (thana) guards, and then proceeded through Kodimeh and Rāçānapalleh, and arrived at Zantulūr: there he demanded that the garrison (thāna) should surrender. But as the (killadar) commandant of the place did not submit, he scaled the walls and slew the commandant, and placed another captain instead. Thence he marched through Reddipalleh, Reculakoonta, and Siddarama puram, and Uppara palleh and arrived at Rāptād.

At this place all the people in the town came out to meet him with great rejoicings, and carried Basavapa Nayu into the town.

7. Now it so happened that Bharmaji Dalava and Sultanji Dalava, commandants in the service of the Ghorpadeh [a certain Mahratta chieftain] along with Chinnaji, were, at the head of sixty horse, an elephant and (nagara)‡ drums, marching on their way to Murari Rao, who was at Trichinopoly, with a view to enter his service: they halted at the bank of the Rāptād rivulet.

Then Mecala Chinnaii, accompanied by the Reddis (head farmers) and karnams (village clerks) waited on these personages; they had

---

* That is Ramapa the red (or fair complexioned) shepherd.

† That is, "the village on the rock."

‡ The Nagara is the drum that is granted as a mark of honour.

an interview with Bharmaji and asked "Who are you, and whence do you come?" He told all their story(ª): and on [the Reddis] hearing it, and reporting the matter to their (dhanī) chieftain Basavappa; he on hearing their words again sent the same Mecala Chinnaiia, and summoned those three (Sardars) captains, and gave them an interview: he said I have a small affair* on hand: you shall at once receive your pay for four months: or else I will pay you small sums on account.† As soon as my business is carried through, I will give you suitable wages‡ and fitting villages for dividends:§ and will retain you here. If you will support me at this time, you shall have bread as long as the family stands.

So saying he caused some respectable men (pedda manushulu) to speak with them and by God's mercy (Sri Deva cripa) the [captains] gave their promise and remained here in the service. He gave them (tankha) assignments on the revenue, payable monthly (al al hissab) on account.

Basava then took the cavalry, and the footmen whom he had assembled, and laid close siege to Bucca Raya Samudram.

8. Then Zaggulu Mallappa, and Rama Chandra Nayac, and Kurugodu Surappa and Junja Bhai the Turk, (who belonged to Ramapa of Bellari and were at Anantapuram,) all four took counsel and [wrote a letter to his master Ramapa Nayac at Bellary to this effect. [Z]

"Bucca raya Samudram is closely besieged: the old troops there, the head farmers and the clerks, have ruined the villages, and gone over to Basavappa. As soon as they have seized this village, they are likely to come to Anantapuram. In this village as we are new inhabitants, there is no one who will answer when we call. If there-

---

(ª) Page 41.

* Rāçakaryam: literally a Rāça affair, knightly matters, that is, a battle: the Rāça varu (vulgarly Ratswars) were the old barons.

† Al-al-hissab على الحساب an Arabic phrase, "on account," or, per share.

‡ Tsambalam: Shambelam (சம்பளம் Tamil,) pay, wages.

§ Ummalige (Kannadi ಉಮ್ಮಳಿಗೆ for participation. One of the many words wanting in Reeve's Karnataca Dictionary.

fore [you] at this time will make a rapid march with all your troops, fall upon them and raise the siege, we shall again see your face. If you fail on this occasion, to come, our fate is in God's hands. [Z]"

He dispatched this letter by express* and sent it by the hand of Munei Vira Bhadrudu. The moment that the baron of Bellary read this letter, he sent for the troops at Kurugodu and Bellari, and gave them to the charge of his younger brother Hanumapa Nayu and sent them saying, "You are to go and fall upon them and raise the siege and return." They [accordingly] went (lit. *came*) and three hours after noon they assaulted the troops of Basavapa who were closely beleaguering the place: (ᵃ) a great battle took place between them and many were slain on each side. Then Basavapa's men withdrew from the siege, and going along the inner (bank) of the tank, [they fled] along the Upparla palli road† and taking refuge behind the Gummana embankment, they halted in Belappa's grove. The Bellary troops then returned to Anantapuram.

9. When the Nabob of Karpa‡ heard of these brawls, he considered that an ancient family was now in difficulties for want of allies. He therefore gave some troops into the hand of a captain (sardar) who was with him, saying, You are to march with speed, and chase away the Bellari chiefs who are in that village; you are to garrison Anantapuram: and write me a report of your doing this. The [Kadapa] captain set out, and halted on the bank of the Kōtaleru stream near Narpala. When the Bellary captains in the fort heard of this, they thought "They must have written to the [Nabob of] Kadapa to fall upon us." They and their troops were in consternation; their army broke up and fled to Rāptād and thereabouts; then they departed every man to his village.

10. When baron Basavapa heard this news, he arose, with (his captain) Bharmaji, (see above) and halted at Rāptādu. When the

---

* Literally, (Khaddi katti) "he tied a bit of wood to the letter."—this denoted that it was to travel with speed. Compare the Lady of the Lake, verse 8 canto 3; "a slender crosslet, a cubit's length in measure," was the similar rite used in the highlands.

(ᵃ) Page 42.

† Lit: the village of the Diggers. The uppara vandlu are the tribe who do the work of excavators. In England they are called Navigators.

‡ Probably Majid Khan who was Nabob of Cuddapa in AD. 1753.

Bellari garrison *in the fort* heard that Basavapa's forces had retired, they were alarmed and considered thus: "Probably [Basavapa's troops] have gone to meet the Oudapa troops, to bring them also and to-morrow night they will assault our town: in the fight yesterday many were slain: and there was no opportunity to carry off the dead. In this state of things, if the other army should come, we have no resource." Accordingly the men who were in Anantapuram and in Buccaraya Samudram, taking along with them these four captains, fled by night to Topudurru: which they reached at dawn of day. So they returned to Bellari.

As these two villages [Anantapuram and Buccasamudram] were burnt down and desolate, three men named, Timmaiia of the almanacks, Sarabha the Tambali who was priest to Saint Virabhadra, with Beau-Racer* the herb seller, came into the village to look after and carry off their goods [among the ruins]: then Sarabha returned with all speed to Rāptād(*) and said to Basava:—"There is not a soul in Bucca Raya Samudram: it is desolate and burnt down: all the people have quitted the village and fled. You should come speedily with your troops [and possess the place."]

11. At this time four Jangams, disciples of Siva Linga Devara,† at the Gavi monastery (matham) which was on the black hillock under the bank of the Anantapur tank, came to the Ambassador's sluice for oleander flowers, [which they required] for the purpose of celebrating the worship of Siva. They saw all the populace flying out of Anantapuram bearing their bundles, along the bank of the tank: they heard it said that the Bellari people had fled by midnight out

---

* "Gidda Paru vu-gadu:" perhaps a cant name: but some men bear ludicrous names from infancy.

(*) Page 43.

† This name denotes, "the blessed image of Baal-Peor:" but here, is a man's name. The Lingam is adored as the *Destroyer*, not, as some European writers fancy, the Reproducer. The rites are always gloomy and austere: and have nothing indecent or obscene. The Hindus have no belief in the existence of the Devil: but Siva, or the Lingam seems to be a deity exactly analogous to Satan. This however is quite distinct from the *Pei-puja*, or Devil worship which prevails in Tinnevelly. When the Bramins introduced the worship of Vishnu in Southern India, about A. D. 1100, they abolished the demon-worship (with human sacrifices) as far as their power extended.

of [Anantapuram] fort:" the [Jangams] returned and related this to St. Sivalinga. He set out accompanied by the Jangam sages, who were with him, and visited the fort of Anantapuram. The opened gates still stood open. He closed the doors: he dipt an old cloth in turmeric,* fastened it on the beam of a lance, and put it on the Tiger's face [carved in stone over the fort gate], placing there an old drum which [the fugitives] had left [behind them]. Then he had the drum beaten, and said "This fort† now belongs to Handē Sidda Ramapa," [who was formerly imprisoned in fetters.] And then he sent a Jangam to desire Basavapa to bring his troops.

12. When Basava was [first] informed by the Tambali Sarabha [see section 10] who came from Bucca Raya Samudram, of what had happened, he gave some men to Chinnaiia-of-the-goats, and ordered him to accompany the Tambali Sarabha to Bucca Raya Samudram: which he was directed to garrison. But he himself marched with his troops towards Anantapuram. On the road the Jangam [messenger] met him and told him the news. He was delighted and said "Surely Saint Sidda Rameswara‡ has now been gracious to us." He came with speed and garrisoned Anantapuram: while Chinnaiia-of-the-goats marched to Bucca Raya Samudram and garrisoned that place. Thus both villages were garrisoned.

13. Meantime the troop who had come from Kadapa [see No. 9] and had halted on the banks of the Nārpula stream, arose and proceeded on to Our Lady's Square:§ then, on enquiring into the condition of the [two] forts, [the Cuddapa captain] heard it said, "To day Basavappa([a]) son-in-law of the late Ramapa Nayu [the laird of Anantapuram, who was assasinated, [see chap. IV. No. 7] has

---

* Turmeric is always emblematic of good tidings.

† Lit: it has become his (Thanyam) garrison. This word is the Marata Thana, with an illiterate affix.

‡ The saint whose image he carried away from Anantapuram: See chapter IV. No. 10.

§ Amma Varu, the Madonna, or mother-goddess. That is Durga or Kali, that is Cotytto. This saint is the inflicter of the small pox, which is named after her.

([a]) Page 44.

come with a sufficient force, and garrisoned both villages." On hearing this he halted there that night.

When Basavapa in the fort heard these tidings, he said to Devanna the (desai) commandant: "Go by night, enter [their] camp, wait upon the captains, and say, By the goodness of God (Sri Devuni cripa valla) the village is again in our hands: hereafter* we will act according to your directions: tell them all the details, and return." So saying he dismissed [Devanna] who accordingly marched and spoke to the captains (sardārlu) who were well pleased that the goods had now returned to the hand of the owner: then they arose and went home to Karpa.

14. During these troubles,† the bank of the Buccapatnam Tank had burst near (Nalla guṭṭala) the Black hills. Basavappa Nayadu granted there new (cowl) leases to two villages, and also to the district, and increased the population: he went about from village to village, encouraging the villagers: he bestowed vestments and vessels upon them, and caused them to carry on cultivation.

15. Six months passed thus. The (subedar) commandant of Hirehāl,‡ and the commandant of Kuditini, both wrote reports to [their master] Murari Rao [the Mahratta chieftain]. On reading these he was much pleased, [and in reply he wrote a letter and sent it to them, wherein he said"] "Take good care of Sidda Ramappa, and as soon as a letter is received from Basavapa written from Anantapuram, give [Sidda Rama] as a present, suitable clothes, vessels, and some men to accompany him; so send him home to [his] village." [Z]

16. Such being the case, Basavappa strengthened his dominion at Anantapuram and wrote to the two Subedars, Sivappa and Zantangi Rao of Kuditini, that on the day of the full moon in the month Margasira, when the car festival to Saint Virupaxa takes place, the astral hour will be lucky for crowning, &c. [the young laird Siddappa]; adding details of all he was doing there. Both of them, on receiv-

---

* Mundu: literally, *before*.

† In the original read I'calāpana lo': in these &c.

‡ The fallen chief, Sidda Ramaya was still in the house of Sivappa, the ruler of Hirchal. See sections 1 and 2 of chapter V. regarding Murari Rao, see chap. II.

ing the letter, (according to the orders received from Murari Rao regarding this) sent for Sidda Ramapa who was in the fort([a]) [of Hirehāl]: they presented him with suitable clothes, vessels, &c., with some horses and men, and sent him to Anantapuram.

17. Then [raja] Sidda Ramapa set out from thence, on the 9th of the crescent moon in Margasira [4th Dec. 1753]. On the 12th he reached Korakolla, and next day came to Kūdēru where he halted. Next day the 14th of the light fortnight [Sunday 9th Dec. 1753] he [meaning Basavapa] performed the feast to Saint Sangam Eswar: and on the [next day] full moon, in a fortunate hour at noon, at the time when the (vadam) cables of his majesty the god's car were laid hold of,* Basavapa with his men and horsemen issued from the village, and met the procession at Cats-mount (pilli gutta) to the west of Anantapuram: he conveyed Sidda Ramapa along and caused him to behold the god during the time of the car procession; then conveying him into the fort, he seated [the raja] on the throne, while soldiers, militia, and ministers all paid their homage: and [the Protector] bestowed vests and tambūlams [see No. 1 chap. V.] appropriately, and ushered [them] into the (petta) town. Thence Sidda Ramappa proceeded into the palace. This was in the year Srimukha. [SS. 1675. A. D. 1753.] On that day he was crowned king of the realm.† He appointed his brother-in-law, Cari-huli Basavappa as his (dalavai) General. Thus he ruled the country. After a short time he caused the breach to be repaired which was made in the bank of the Buccapatnam tank.

CHAPTER SIXTH.

1. Afterwards, in a few days, Murari Rao [the Marata general] of Gutti gave two thousand horse, and four thousand foot to Elias

---

([a]) Page 45.

* The cables by which the people drag the car of a god. Vadam is a Tamil word for the Telugu *moku*. Virgil says *Gaudent tractare rudentes*. All the verbs, set out, reached, &c. are, in the original, participles: *having* set out, &c.

† Some of the Saxon kings ruled states not larger than the "realm" here described.

Khan and said to him, "Go thou to Anantapuram, and collect for me the outstanding balance of tribute* due to us." So he marched with his troops and besieged Bucca Raya Samudram: and demanded the outstanding balance of tribute. They replied "What do we [now] possess? [The] family has but lately again come [to the throne]; it is well known to his highness Murari Rao." In this way they earnestly entreated the captain(a) who had come: he replied, After we have come and taken our stand here, it is not fit to send us away without† paying.

Then they agreed that ten thousand rupees should be paid: [to make up this sum] they surrendered all the bullocks and pack saddles that were in the palace: all the (sāmān) stuff and leathern bottles (of oil) and some money; all this was delivered to [the demanders] and the whole amounted to four thousand rupees. There were six thousand rupees still due as a balance; so they levied a poll tax on all the people in the town at the rate of five pagodas per head: they raised it through [the responsibility of] Krishnama the shopkeeper of Kandukur and paid it. Then the troops arose and went to besiege Dharmavaram.

2. Afterwards this Sidda Ramapa called for Baiiana-gāri Anantaiia (see chap. V. No. 4) and very graciously bestowed vests and vessels on him, saying "Thou hast exerted thyself greatly for us;" After shewing him every kindness, he lastly gave him, in payment of his debt, the (Upparla palleh) "Navigators‡ village:" and also wrote a document conferring upon him a half share in the Bramin village. Likewise bestowing on him the house belonging to Zaggula Mallappa, inside the fort, [as a punishment for Mallappa's treachery and the murder of this baron's father, and the imprisonment of the present ruler. [See chap. III. No. 18. 20.] Then he sent for the captain Bharmaji, the Dalavai (or commandant) and enquired into the length of [his] service: then he gave a (tankha) assignment on

* Chauthai: a quarter: that is, twenty-five per cent. of the collected revenues. The usual Marata phrase for tribute.

(a) Page 46.

† Urikeh, in vain, emptily.

‡ I confess I do not know why diggers and excavators are now in England called *Navigators*.

this Baiianna-gari-Anantaiia, for the balance of his pay, after deducting the (al-al-hissa)* share due to him. And likewise bestowed on him in free gift the village Govindu palle in the Bucca Raya Samudram country.

3. After some more time had passed, in the year Iswara (A. D. 1757) Balavant Rao came with (some) troops and besieged Anantapuram. [The besiegers] placed one battery at the perfumer's shop in the suburbs: and one on the Mallappa bank, and [a third] in the town: they did not even suffer a kitten to move its paw, and used great violence. As Basava had now no money to offer to them to reconcile them, he resolved, saying, Let us fall on this army and die. So he called together his Laird (Siddappa) and the high officers and all the people: and addressed them saying "As we have nothing to offer to these (tyrants) and pacify them, let me to-morrow go at noon, assault their batteries, fight them, and clear the town of them. If I return here, well: otherwise look out for yourselves." So saying he assembled all the troops and said "There is a scheme for the ruin of this family. We have no wealth to offer [to the enemy] and make peace.([a]) Our family is celebrated for (xãtra dharmam) heroism, according to the usual report of us. Let us go at noon to-morrow and fall upon their host, wage battle, remove the batteries, and clear the suburbs: this is the thought of my heart. Let every man who wishes to fight along with me come to me after breakfast to-morrow morning, and wearing yellow robes† let them come and be ready at the sally port near the stone gate of the town."

That night, at four hours‡ [after midnight] he went into the Mansion and ate. Then he visited all the guards and sentries.

4. As it now dawned, he again went into the Mansion: he bathed and caused two great lamps§ to be put before saint Siddha Ram-

* Al-al-hissa. See note. p. 46 The payments made *pro rata*.

([a]) Page 47.

† That is, having smeared their cloths with turmeric because they were devoting their lives as a sacrifice.

‡ Tasu. A Hindu hour: *four hours* denotes about midnight. This reckoning is not now in use.

§ Akhandam: entire: not separated. This is the name given to a lamp which is kept continually burning in a shrine.

Eswara, besides the usual candles in the chapel: he worshipped (Sri Deva) the blessed god: he dressed himself in yellow, and took his farewell* of the laird and of the ministers.

Then he securely arranged† the guards at the fort: he sat down under the margosa tree at the sally port of the stone gate of the town: he called his troops: and taking with him four hundred trust worthy followers, at noon he caused the Kattulūr gate to be unbolted. He rushed out with speed: he assaulted the battery at the Perfumer's shop: he fought stoutly: he set the battery on fire: then he attacked the battery at Saint Mallappa's pagoda which was on the bank; there he slew many: he also burnt down this battery and went straight into the (petta) suburbs: when Balavant Rao in his camp heard this uproar in the town, he summoned some officers and soldiers, (sepoys and sirdars) and said to them: "Go into the town and attack those who have sallied from the fort: chase them again into the fort: and bring me as many as fall into your hands."

5. Accordingly the [Mahrattas] captains and sepoys, stood ready: they went through the Kuderu gate and when they arrived at Saint Virupaxa's chapel in the market, [they found that] the men who were in the fort had cleared out the two batteries and were fighting in the market place. A sharp action took place between them. As many balls and arrows were pouring from the fort, the suburbs being small, the [Marata] troops could not stand their ground: they were broken and fled as far as the Washer's Green. A furious engagement now took place: (a) and the corpses lay in heaps. Basavappa's troops took shelter in the depôt‡ of the Kuderu gate. As it was now evening the whole of Balavant Rao's troops retired [into their] own camp.

6. "When Balavant Rao heard all these tidings he exclaimed "What a (small) fort! what a (stout) power! Many lives are lost." [He] planned to make an assault in the morning. But Bavakhan

* Literally, Spoke: that is uttered his dying words.

† In all this paragraph, the original uses not verbs but past participles: having arrayed, having sat, having called. &c.

(a) Page 48.

‡ عرابة araba, a magazine.

'Halali' and some other captains on Murari Rao's side said to Balavant Rao "If we assault and master this petty fortalice, we shall gain ruined walls alone: there is nothing else. This is an ancient family: they were sunken, and now by [your lordship's] favour it has become a house. He looks to your grace and is a fit object for your mercy. It is said that from the days of his grandfather and great grandfather this house was known for bravery. If you command us to storm the place we will storm it; they will lose their lives: we will act according to your pleasure."

On hearing these words Balavant Rao (daiva yogam cheta) by the will of God called for Kesiva Rao, the agent (vakīl) of Soudekuppam, [who was there] and said to him "Go you, early in the morning, and visit this Basavappa Nayac; reassure him and bring him here with you."

7. Accordingly this Kesiva Rao came into the town betimes in the morning and sent for the chief men who were at the bank of the ditch, (near) the (jībi) "intervallum,"* and said to them, "I am the (vakīl) messenger sent by Balavant Rao: I come from the camp: and I want to speak to Basavappa Nayac. If therefore he (literally, They) will come to the great bank, at the Turkish Tombs, I will speak face to face and all shall be made known. Tell him this and come back."—They went and carried these tidings to Basavappa Nayac. He replied, "Never mind: I will come to the Tiger-face-bastion: and if his honour (lit: They) too will do me the favour to come to the front of the (jībi) *intervallum* we may accordingly converse together." Such was his (badl) reply.

Then this Kesiva Rao came to the terrace which was on the inner bank of the ditch in front of the (jibi) intervallum and sat upon it. Basavappa Nayac also came from inside the fort, and mounted on the tower.† Then they‡ saw each other from afar.

---

* Jībi (Hind جیب) The intervallum or space between the outer and inner wall of a fort. This is noticed in the Kannadi Dictionary, but omitted in the Hindustani Dictionary, printed in 1849. From the context I doubt this interpretation.

† The word is ఊడెము ūdem which seems to be Kannadi.

‡ Lit: those and these.

8. Then ([a]) Kesiva Rao said to Basavappa, "my Laird (Dhani) has given permission* and has desired [me] to bring you to visit him." Basava listened, and replied, "you are [chiefs commanding] a large force: I am a petty (pālēgādu) laird; how am I to be assured of your keeping good faith? We, with our (putra-mitra-calatra-adulu) sons, allies and wives, and with all our kinsmen have girt our loins and are prepared†: as this is the case, I request you to report all these circumstances to their lordship [i. e. to his honour:] and whatever command is given us, provided our lives are not threatened, we will come to wait upon him." So he spoke. Then Kesiva Rao went into the army, and reported to Balavant Rao the resolute reply of Basavappa. On hearing it (he) asked the opinion of the gentlemen (pedda manushulu) present. [They replied saying[1]] "They have lost all hope: and therefore use such desperate language. If you send any respected leader from here, after he enters their fort, and remains there, he (Basava) will come out and have an interview with you. Such is the thought that arises in our minds. But we will act according to your pleasure." [z]

9. Accordingly [Balavant Rao] gave an officer of rank to accompany Kesiva Rao: and the order was that he should be placed in the fort and Basavappa should be brought. Accordingly this Kesiva Rao took that high officer along with him, and came to the front of the (jibi) circumvallation, and sent word of this by some principal persons who were there. They went [into the fort] and reported it: they brought Basavappa outside the (jībī) walls, and an interview took place.

Kesiva Rao repeated all that his master had commanded him to say: and his honour Basavappa was content: he carried the captain with him and placed him in the fort. He himself went into the (nagari) Mansion and reported to the laird and to (Samayajaculu) the managers, and to the ladies, all that took place. He secured the fort, and then he [Basavappa] directed that the (naubat) great drums

---

([a]) Page 49.

* Selavu: leave, or command.

† Lit: Vīrā Kankanam: the bracelet worn by heroes: the mark that they were bound to vanquish or to die.

should be sounded on the tower, and came out with four hundred of his stoutest warriors.

Then he said to Kesava Rao, [I have] another request to make. What is that, replied he. Basavappa replied, "I am unable to go with this petty force into [your] army and have an interview: if his honour Balavant Rao will come to the chapel of Saint Basava in the suburbs, (a) I will come and pay my respects."

10. Accordingly Kesava Rao went and presented this request, and brought Balavant Rao to the Saint's chapel [in the suburbs:] and sent word to his honour Basavappa, who came with his attendants and waited upon [Balavant Rao.] He represented every thing, both good and bad: and got a decision that the tribute claimed should be sixty thousand Rupees. He then took leave* and came home. Then he took the great chieftain who had been placed in the fort [as a hostage:] and brought him into the (diwan) great hall, where he prepared a capital supper for him, presented vests, vessels and tambulam (see page 42,) and stated all his own adventures, adding "We now look to you for the restoration of this House." Then giving him leave, he sent him [back] to the [Marata] army.

This (jamadar) captain went and saluted [his master], who asked the state of things in the fort. He replied "The men of this family are men of valour, not men of wealth. They are men of large families: they are fit objects for your mercy." The three main points were represented, and he added "Henceforth we shall act according to your [honour's] pleasure." So saying he took leave and went to his tent.

11. Afterwards this Basavappa clearly made known to his liege lord Sidda Ramappa and to his counsellors all the particulars of his having gone to Balavant Rao, and having had an interview, and having agreed regarding the money. He then took leave.

Next day he gave directions to the guard to fire at any of Balavant Rao's men who might roam round the fort and the town. Accordingly the men on the fort fired balls among them. When Balavant Rao heard of this, he sent for Kesiva Rao and said "It appears that the

---

(a) Page 50.

* Appana is a Kannadi word, much used in Telugu.

truce [we] made last night is broken; go thou therefore to the fort, and learn [the state of things."] So Kesava Rao came to the front of the fort, and sent for Basavappa. He asked, "as peace was made yesterday, what means the firing balls to-day?" Basavappa replied, "we have no means of paying you the money. (a) To make another bargain would be a degradation.* We accordingly wished to depart to (vīra swargam) the heaven of heroes, with our sons, friends and relations. We therefore threw a cannon ball [into your camp."]

12. On hearing this, Kesiva Rao went and represented this to Balavant Rao. And the sardar (captain) who had gone out of the fort the day before also pleaded, with him then for Basavappa. [Balavant Rao] listened and smiled and said to Kesava Rao "we have struck off ten thousand Rupees and agree to take fifty thousand. If this is paid we will march off. Tell Basava Nayac this."

Accordingly Kesava Rao went to Basava and said, what say you about the 50,000 Rupees? He replied, pray your lord to do me the favour to wait till to-morrow and I will pay it. So having sent back [Kesiva Rao], he sold all the valuables that were in his mansion, which amounted to four thousand rupees. As Modeen Saheb, son-in-law to Bawa Khan, (Subedar) commandant under Murari Rao was in service here [i. e. under Basava,] Basava sent for him through some respectable men in order to raise funds, and said "I rely on you in some way or other to rescue my family." The man replied "There shall be wanting no endeavour on my part to relieve you." Basava replied, I beg (*v.*) you to advance me ten thousand rupees to satisfy the army: [that is, to pay Balavant Rao.]

"What matters it?" replied he: "if the family stands, you will certainly repay me.†" Accordingly [Modeen Saib] caused a bond to be executed in Sidda Ramappa Nayac's name, countersigned by Basavappa [as minister], and thus raised and paid ten thousand rupees.

13. The next day Kesiva Rao came and asked Basavappa 'what is your answer about the money?' 'I will at present' replied he

---

(a) Page 51.

* Paurusha-hani: loss of respectability.

† Observe the phrase Iyyanē iççeru.

'pay 14,000 rupees, and for the balance, rupees 36,000, I will mortgage my [village named] New Tank. I request that after having received the balance due, you will persuade (Balavant Rao) to give up the village." So Kesiva Rao went back to head quarters and reported this to Balavant Rao, who consented. Then [Kesiva Rao] came back and took the 14,000 rupees in coin, ([a]) and [the deeds mortgaging] the village. He carried his honour Basava four miles along with him, and then gave him leave to return to the fort, with every mark of consideration, bestowing upon him according to the ancient custom a dress* of honour, with a horse, and equipments. Afterwards Basavappa having returned to the fort with all these gifts, laid them before his Master Sidda Ramapa, who was much pleased. Next day the army broke ground and marched by the Parlapallē road.

14. Basavappa Nayudu let out the waste lands under special agreements and caused the tillage to be increased: and after collecting the revenue due on the crops reaped in the month Kartica, he sent to Balavant Rao, by means of Bava Saheb, the sum still due, being 36,000 rupees. Whereupon he [Balavant Rao] recalled the officers [whom he had appointed to hold the mortgaged lands] at New tank.

Afterwards, Basavappa Nayudu set this village to rights, and superintended the whole realm [or barony.]

Formerly while he [Basavapa] was passing from Bellari to Vemula, (see chapter V. No. 5) on his way, he halted near Pamudurti, and sent and asked for grass, firewood, and other articles from Yoganandam, the master of Ellutla in the Tadimarri district, who was then in that village; but that person treated the message with contempt, and said "these things are not to be had here." And he sent away the messengers without.† [Basavappa] laid this up in his heart. He set out on horseback under cover of night, and rapidly reached Ellutla, which was more than ten coss from Anantapuram. Just as it was dawning he halted in the chapel of Saint Hanumant, in the suburbs. He there seized upon Yoganandam, with his cattle and his people: and plundered the village.

([a]) Page 52.

* Sir-pao (Hind) a dress from head to foot, that is, Turban, trowsers, jacket, belt and sash.

† Uraca—Here it means 'empty-handed.'

15. And as he was coming along, Ramapa Nayu, laird of Tadimarri, heard of this, and set out with his horse and foot and met [Basavappa] in the road. A combat took place, and the Tadimarri troop was worsted. So [Basavappa] returned (safe) to Anantapuram. There he sold all the (lifted) cattle and levied a fine upon his prisoners (for ransoms.) He secured (his prisoner) Yoganandam in the fort, and mulcted him in the sum of four thousand rupees:* then bestowing honorary vests and the *tambulam* on him, [Basava] sent him home again to Tadimarri.

Besides (a) when this Basavappa had formerly taken leave of Sivappa, the baron of Hirehal, (see chapter V. 3.) and was returning home, he halted at noon near the Nimbacallu well: and as there were no worshippers of Siva† present to cook his food for him, but there was of old some acquaintance between his fathers, and Muddu Mallappa, the (Desai) Master of Hoosoor, (see the beginning of chapter third) he sent for some food to Immadacca [a daughter of Mallappa's family], and she [instead of sending him food] sent back a scornful message.

By reason of some occurrences of that time,‡ the head watchman of that village was discontented,§ and was come to Anantapuram in quest of employ: and the folks here brought him to Basavappa. When [they were] writing down his features, they asked "what is thy name? which is thy village?" He replied, "my name is O'badū: my village is Nimbacallu. I am the head watchman‖ of that place." Then [Basavappa] recollecting the scornful language used by Ima-

* The Hindus exclaim greatly against the cruelties of the Musulman conquerors. But these stories shew us how the Hindus treated each other. Their rajas were as lawless and cruel as the old barons in England.

(a) Page 53.

† Meaning, Jangam: the caste to which he belonged. See page 301 of the Telugu Dictionary, and page 574 regarding their leader Basavappa after whom the hero of this story is named: as are many persons at the present day.

‡ The phrase is Sanscrit: *kala desa vartamanam*, literally by reason of the circumstances of time and place.

§ Aluguta: this verb in ancient Telugu meant to be enraged, to be wroth. In modern days it denotes discontent, slight anger, annoyance.

‖ The Talāri was the hereditary bailiff, executioner, and watchman.

dacca, enlisted this man and increased his pay, desiring him to come and visit him daily.

16. While the watchman was thus in his service, he one day called this Obadu secretly, and told him clearly all the story about Imadacca. He added, if you will put the village [of Nimbacallu] into my power I will reward you. He pressed him much: whereupon [Obadu] went twice or thrice into that village, and inspected its state, and returned to Basavappa. Then he carried Basavappa to the village of Cūdēru, by way of a stroll,* and halted there for one day. He assembled the people of the village, and raised a mob. Hence he made a rapid journey by night to Nimbacallu, and utterly plundered that village: he carried off both the cattle and the inhabitants. He seized [dame] Imadacca and returned to Kūdēru. He levied fines on the tenants, and realized some money, and assigned over the rest of the money to his soldiers. He sold off the cattle and the sheep,† and collected the money. He carried off Imadacca to Anantapuram.

When Cari Ramappa, laird (desai) of Hosoor, heard of this, (a) he wrote letters to Basavappa, begging him to look back‡ to their common ancestors, and send back dame Imadacca. He sent [this message] by the hands of fit and respectable messengers. When Basavappa had read the letters, he exacted four thousand Rupees from Imadacca, and having presented her honourable gifts, and having also rewarded O'badu the watchman [for his treachery], and having pacified her, he sent her with him home to their town.

17. Afterwards, Murari Rao [the Marata general] of Gutti was marching through (Upparla palli) Navigators-town on his way to Penugonda, plundering the villages on his way. He halted near Bomma parti, and Basavappa, on hearing of it, summoned the (sipahilu) troops in his own employ. He said [The Marata] has

---

* *Swāri* meant for (H) Sawari, an excursion on horse back.

† Sheep are rarely mentioned as wealth by the Hindus in the country where these occurrences took place. Immense flocks are reared solely for the purpose of manuring land: and to this end the flocks are hired out to farmers who fold the sheep on their fields.

(a) Page 54.

‡ Lit: to keep an eye on the elders.

plundered my crops to the amount of ten thousand rupees; go and plunder the mixed multitude that follows his army.

They started, and as he ordered, they plundered his horse, camels, and forage,* and returned to Anantapuram.

When Murari Rao heard of this, he sent his (vakeel) agent Parangi † Tammanna with a message, saying; if you have suffered loss by my troops, deduct the value out of the sum due to me as my quarter share of the (revenue). And thus he released the horses, camels and cattle, which Basava's men had seized.

Afterwards Basava dug a well in the name of his elder sister Nilamma, on the Cūdēru road, a quarter of an hour to the west of Anantapuram. He planted a grove of bilva and other trees.

CHAPTER SEVENTH.

1. After some days,‡ [a captain] named Mīr Sayad-ulla Khan went from the Nawab Bahādar Hyder Ali Khan, marching to make an attack§ in the neighbourhood of Gurramconda: he came by the Tadimarri road to Anantapur: all the army halted half a coss west of the town, in the mid-stream.‖ The van (agārī fauj) extended to Virapa's pagodas. Basavappa (a) spied them from the top of the [Anantapuram] fort. He said "the army is encamping in order to besiege the town. Fire at them with cannon ball." This was done: and in consequence some shop tents, some people, a flag and other things were swept away.

On hearing of this Mir Sayad-ulla Khan (the commandant) was much incensed: he begirt the town, but for four days each party sat

* Kavār: a Dakhini word, given in the Tamil Dictionary. This shews that they seized the sinews of war alone.

† Parangi may either mean *Cannon:* or *European:* an instance of family names originating in nick names.

‡ The rest of the history abounds with Hindustani words.

§ Mohim مهم a raid or inroad.

‖ This word Midstream is perhaps the name of a village, Nadimi-vanca.

(a) Page 55.

still. He sent by his vakeel from the army [to Basavappa] demanding payment of the (peshcush) tribute due: on payment of which he promised that the force should draw off. The (vakil) messenger came and stated this to his honour Basavappa, who thereupon sent his vakeel Murarappa-gari, Rangappa, and Bōlē Khan: they went to the besieging ruler, and had an interview (sawal-jawab), and settled that an impost (Khandini) of 30,000 rupees should be submitted to. And in security for the payment thereof, (Basava) gave the two ambassadors as (olu) hostages. Afterwards the troops marched away.

After two months he sent the money to the invader, and recalled his two hostages, Bōlē Khan and Rangapa.

2. Afterwards, the laird of Tadimarri, (see chap. vi. 14.) who had kept in his mind his former sorrow on account of his village Ellutla having been sacked, and Yoganandum carried off, [in revenge] invaded the country of Anantapuram and plundered it. On account of this, Basavappa attacked and plundered the [Tadimarri] barony. Ramappa Nayudu of Tadimarri (the foster son of lady Nandemma,) being incensed at this, marched with his troops into the neighbourhood of Pasuloor: there he halted; and intending to plunder the Tank diggers town, he took with him the [allies] who were at Pasuloor, and halted near the well at the boundary: and some stragglers from his troops were roving about in quest of cows, and sheep. But the people of Tank diggers town wrote a letter to Basavappa, stating these tidings: whereupon as he marched with his men, horse, foot-soldiers, bowmen, and horse artillery,* to Giriapa's grove, at an hour's distance, on the south east of Tankdiggers town, a sharp action took place between (' these and those') the combatants, and near Doccala gandi many were slain on both sides. The Tadimarri troops were broken, and fled to Pasulūr.

Basavappa then paused from fighting, and blew the trumpet, proclaiming quarter: and gave permission to the Tadimarri people to carry off their dead. (a) He rested for four (ghadis) hours in a mango grove near Tank-diggers town.

---

* This (swāri pirungulu) seems to mean light guns (jinjals) borne on horses.

(a) Page 56.

He heard that they [of Tadimarri] had removed from Pasulūr to Tadimarri, and therefore returned with his troops to Anantapuram. Thus mortal hatred existed, between ('those and these') both of them.

3. Matters standing thus, Vencatapati Nayu of Vēpali came [to visit] the Tadimarri family: he gave bad advice to Ramapa [head of that family], and led him into some bad practices, so that [Ramapa] drank till he lost his senses, and committed outrages in the village. When Basavappa heard of this, he said "this family is fallen into folly, we must set a guard over it." So he gave some troops and horse guns in charge to these two persons, Subarao the clerk (sabnivees) and Rudrapa the Dalavāi (captain) and had them thus in readiness. Musalaiia of Nande-samudram, and Fair-Guruva-of-the hoof, (who had been sent [as spies] to find out the actual state of the Tadimarri fort) returned, saying, "To-day there is neither watch nor guard in the fort. All the troops who were in the suburbs last night, have gone into the woods to follow the chase."

Thereupon [Basavappa] sent these two [spies] with the two (faujdar) captains, and under their orders, [to march to Tadimarri] and ordered them to seize and man the fort and send him word. He sent on quickly his troops beforehand.

4. After day dawned, while Basavappa also was going, the party sent on before came near to Velaparla, and placing ladders, entered the fort. As there was no guard at the gate, and all were careless, [the assaulters] desirous of plunder surrounded the houses in the fort, and were plundering. Arey Syāmanta Rayu, and Dīna the Musulman, and other servants, were sleeping in the upper chambers with Ramapa Nayu. One of them arose for a private purpose, and hearing the hubbub, he came to the palace gate, and heard some women in the fort crying "the Hande clan have seized the fort, have beset the houses and are plundering. We have no protection!" On hearing this, this man went and awoke his master Ramapa Nayu (a) and the other people, and told them. On hearing of it, they armed themselves, and opening the palace gate, repulsed the troops who had come to surround the palace, and fought, till they reached the town gate.

(a) Page 57.

The people of the town, in the suburbs, on hearing the uproar, cried Treason! (lit: Mischief!) armed themselves, and hemmed in the citadel. And as the ladders which the men of Anantapoor had placed and entered the fort with, were left unoccupied (khālī) the townsmen using these ladders secured the guards and keepers of the (alangam) ramparts, of the tower;* thus they hemmed in the Anantapur force, who were in the fort.

5. When [Basavappa's officers] Rudrapa and Subraya who were outside of the fort with some troops, were coming with the troops to the outer suburbs, they perceived that balls were flying over the citadel, and thought "there is Treason! our men are entrapped in the fort!" In the fight that took place inside the citadel between the men of Anantapur and the (sthalam mandi) garrison, many men of the Anantapoor troops fell: the rest forsook their arms, leapt down from the fort, and told Rudrapa and Subraya, who were with the army. They hearing this were much grieved. Then, seeing that the garrison had opened the gate, and, headed by their (dhanī) liege lord, were coming to attack their men, Rudrapa and Subraya cried (Tappenu!) "It has failed!" and then they and their men retreated. Near a hamlet called Ekapādam [literally one-foot-place] beyond the hill fort of Chīyēdu, they met Basavappa Nayu who was advancing. They reported the matter to him; he was much incensed at these (sardārs) captains and said, The fort, which was in our hands, is lost. Then he took the fugitives with him and returned to Anantapuram.

6. From that time fights continually took place between them.† One day Ramapa Nayu, laird of Tādimarri, set out with his men, in broad day light, intending to smite [the village of] Rāptād. He halted‡ near the well in the neighbourhood of Pasulūr, beyond the mango grove of Upparlapalleh.§ The people of that place sent word of this to Basava; and on hearing of it he marched with his (sainyam) army, taking his guns [small cannon] with him; and when he was going to Rāptād, they met him as they were coming from the mango

---

* The *buruzu* (Arabic, *burj*, a bulwark) is the name used for a tower or fortalice.

† Lit. To those and to these.

‡ Lit: depending on the well.

§ Uppara vandlu: tank diggers. Similar to miners.

grove of Upparlapalleh.(ᵃ) A severe fight took place between the two parties and many of the Tadimarri men were slain: they could not stand their ground; and fled leaving behind them two camel guns,* and two baggage camels, and one (nagara wante) camel bearing the kettle drums, and flag: with their sumpter horses (kotal) and other things they went to Pula kunta.

Basavapa blew the trumpet proclaiming quarter (Dharma-dāra-commu) and granted them leave to carry off their dead. He took all the spoil that had fallen into his hands, and went to the mango grove at Miners'town. There he rested from his fatigues. He got intelligence that Kamapa Nayu had fled to Tadimarri: and with his force he returned to Anantapuram.

7. Afterwards, when six months had passed, this Basavappa heard from many persons that [z] Tadipartipeta, twelve coss from Anantapuram, had grown very (basti) populous; and the (Amin) superintendent of that place, Rangu Govindu by name, had traded largely and lent [money] on interest to Murari Rao: and [thereby] had obtained office at Tadiparti [z]. [Basavappa] had for two years had it in his heart to plunder this town, and was looking out for an opportunity to do so. And on the day after the Car-Feast, on the day of the new moon in the month of Magha, he suddenly marched with his men, and set his guards around the town [of Tadiparti] and sent in a Commandant with a few troops to plunder the town. Then with a second party he hemmed in the fort, and by means of ladders descended into it. He set guards around the house of Rangu Govindu Rayu: and as the ten superintendents‡ were there, he seized and secured them: he rushed into the house and seized this Rangu Govindu, and his folk, great and small, with his brother-in-law named Çau-

---

(ᵃ) Page 58.

* Sawari pirangulu are guns conveyed on horses or camels: often called jinjauls: or large match locks.

(z) Here as elsewhere z denotes that the phraseology is inverted, the first line of the original being the last in the translation.

‡ Tahsildar: a superintendent of collectors. A tormentor or exactor See. St. Matthew xviii. 34.

dappa* Nayu, and put them in guard. He searched the house, and carried off silver and gold, some money, some valuable cloths and vestments, brass pots and pans, and plough-cattle, to boot.† Basavappa got all this into his hands. He halted three days in that village. He settled what sums should be levied from merchants, from bramins, from weavers, and others, proportionably, and realized the sums. He carried off whatever he found at hand in the town, money, gold and silver, oxen, (a) and sheep.

When he was returning home with them to Anantapuram, the people who lived round about Tadiparti sent letters to Murāri Rao of Gutti (vulgarly Ghooty) [to come and protect them.]

8. When Murari Rao [the lord baron of the marches] read these letters, he sent for Salih Khan, who was building a fort near Chennam Palli: and told him all that had happened. He said "Go, with some force, and meet Basava Nayak's men on their way, smite them, and set Rangu Govindu and his men at liberty."—Accordingly Salih Khan with his troops marched by the Eccalur road and made enquiries. He learnt that his honour Basavappa had plundered the whole town of Tadiparti and retired by the hill pass near Vencata palleh, proceeding by the 'Mid-hut'‡ road, and had arrived at mid-day in [Handeh] Anantapuram.

On hearing this, he turned back and with his army he arrived [at home in] Gutti. Basavappa brought Rangu Govindu to Anantapur and put him in ward: and levied from him a ransom of 12,000 'Nayus'§ pagodas, and then dismissed him with honorary vestments and vessels.

---

* Or, Samudappa : author of a set of well known ludicrous songs : obscene enough but very popular. They have been printed repeatedly. Some think however the two men are different.

† This story shews how the peaceable innocent Hindus behaved to each other. Such outrages were ended by the Musulman rule : and the cruelties of the Musulmans lasted until it pleased God that the English rule began.

(a) Page 59.

‡ Nadimi doddi : some small hamlet.

§ The *varaha* or gold coin called a pagoda has been at various times of different values. The name *pagoda* is corrupted (says Bartolomeo in his Travels) from *Bhagavati* (Venus) whose figure is stamped upon it. The Hindustani name Hoon is from the Canarese word *honnu* meaning Gold. The Canteroy pagoda is named from 'Kanthirava' or Lion : the title of an ancient raja who ruled Kanara. The 'Nayu' probably denotes' Timma Nayus' coinage.

Again in a few days [Basavapa] marched with his troops to [the village of] Pamudi, plundered Konampeta and returned.

9. After two months had elapsed, Basavappa obtained secret information that there was a rich village named Roddam on the high way at sixteen coss from Anantapuram: he therefore instantly marched there with his troops; when he reached Appaji palleh and Gauram palleh which are about midway, it began to dawn. So he plundered these two villages: and stript some merchants who had halted on the road with a convoy of treacle. He seized the villagers (capulu) and sent a guard with them to Buccapatnam. Meanwhile he set his troops around Putta parti, and appointed Subbarayu and Gubbala Hanumappa as commandants. He left them there and rapidly returned to Anantapuram.

After a fortnight there was an unseasonable fall of rain and the river was flooded. The troops raised the siege and returned to Buccapatnam. They wrote and sent all the news to Anantapuram. But Basavappa on reading it replied 'what business (a) is [to be done] there? arise and come here.' According to this order all these troops returned to Anantapuram.

10. After four months, in the year Khara,* the 14th of the dark fortnight in the month Bhadrapada [that is, 7th Oct. 1771,] a prodigious fall of rain raised the river Chitravati:† the Templestone‡ (Gudibanda) tank burst as well as some others, and the flood passed all bounds: the Buccapatnam tank was filled, and the two sluices being insufficient, the waves poured over the embankment: and as Musalaiia [the tide waiter] had forgotten to heap earth over the broken sluice, the waters rushed through the chasm, and near Blackhills (Nalla gutta) about a hundred fathoms of ground was cut through, and the bank burst. On reading the letter written regarding this by the villagers, Basavappa, who had built a second

---

(a) Page 60.

* In the original the years are marked by Titles alone: no numerals are used.

† The Pennar river falls into the sea near Nelloor. Out of it, between Jammal-madugu and Tadparti, the Chitravati runs southwards.

‡ In a few such names which are of no note, I translate the expressions. Floods like this often happen and cause prodigious loss.

fort at Anantapuram, and prepared store houses for grain, laid aside the work of digging the trench, and with all speed, taking Devanna the head-man with him, reached Buccapatnam. In a fortunate hour he employed men in repairing the breach at the tank. While he was building it, and about three quarters of the work was completed, Basavappa was seized with illness: he mounted in his palankeen and proceeded to Anantapuram, where in a few days the same disease having increased, in the year Khara, month Magha, the 5th of the bright fortnight [9 Feb. 1772] he expired.

11. Afterwards, Sidda Ramappa Nayu caused this Buccapatnam tank to be completely repaired. He kept Subbaraya (still) with him, and ruled the barony.

The Peshwa, and Hyder, Nawab of Seringapatam,* demanded (khandini) tribute: and he was thus disturbed by both at once. Thereupon [Sidda Ramaya] collected all the money, and gold and silver in his country and selling even the horses, paid the money demanded by the Peshwa.†

In the year Manmatha, month Kartica, the 6th day of the bright fortnight [i. e. 30th Oct. 1775] Basalat Jang,‡ commandant of A'davāni (vulgarly Adhoni) came from Seringapatam and laid siege to Bellari. But when his honour [Hyder] Bahadar heard of this, he came with speed, and beset Basalat Jang, whose troops were thrown into confusion. They abandoned all the baggage and fled to A'dhava'ni. Then the Bahadar Nawab [meaning Hyder Ali] garrisoned the fort of Bellari.(*) He heard that Murari Rao [the Marata general] was at Gooty—; he at once marched with his army to Gutti, which he sieged for two or three months, after which Gooty fell into his hands.§

12. Then, (Hyder khan) Bahadar, with a view to exacting the tribute that was due from Anantapuram, sent Kannī Rām the (jamādar) serjeant, and Puṭṭaiia the (harcara) messenger, with fifty horse. These

* Compare the Life of Hyder translated by me from the Marata original.

† "The Peshwa" was the title borne by the chieftain who led the armies of the Mahrattas.

‡ See Index to 2d vol. of Orme.

(*) Page 61.

§ Literally, became a garrison.

he placed here on duty. He seized Murari Rao and sent him away by the Anantapuram road: while himself marched with his troops by the Kudēru route, towards Chitracallu. He gave the command of the district of Gooty to Balaji Rao, desiring him to collect Rs. 40,000 a year from the district of Anantapuram. They accordingly continued paying this money, though not regularly.* Thus the Family fell into poverty. At this time Balaji Rao died: and the Gutti district then was committed to Narasappa the (subedar) commandant. In year Plava, month Sravana, the 2d day of the bright fortnight [23d July 1781,] his rule began.

13. He placed his garrison and ruled over all that district. He sent his messengers to distrain for money on the Anantapuram lands. He mercilessly closed the gates of the fort and the doors of the mansion-house and exercised much severity. As they had no money to pay, this Subadar Narasappa sent a clerk named Bettadi Rayu: directing that to prevent the loss of money due by the people of the place, this man should seat† Sidda Ramapa Nayu [the helpless laird]: and, (said he) "you are to look to everything, and write me tidings." Thus he sent this clerk: who on coming, and learning all the state of things, wrote a reply saying 'there are no resources in the country, nor is there any cash in the treasury.'

On receiving this letter, Narasappa came with some troops; he halted near the head man's garden. He sent for [the luckless baron] Sidda Ramapa from the fort and had an interview with him. Narasappa alighted in the house of Timmanna the (sabnivees) recorder, in the suburbs. The laird then took leave and went to his mansion.

14. Next day, Narasappa the commandant went into the fort, and said, 'If you will pay us what is due to us we will go away: what way [have you for paying] the money?' (*) Thus he questioned his honour Sidda Ramappa, who replied "we have no means of paying the money [demanded]. Look after your possession yourselves." So saying he delivered up the keys and the seals of the fort.

---

* Lit: before and after:—a little before or after.

† In such passages, *to seat* means, to arrest a man and never to let him stir from under the tormentors until the sum demanded is paid. This was one of the primitive customs of the Hindus.

(*) Page 62.

Narsappiia replied, If you will pay the money which you have, we will return to Gutti. It is not fit to surrender us the place at present instead of making arrangements according to the state of the times and of the realm. But [Sidda Ramaia] would not listen [to him] and surrendered, saying To pay what you demand is altogether out of my power.

So [Narsappa] secured the fort with guards, appointing one Shekh Mēera as commandant of the fort (Killedar), and committing the affairs of the country to Bettada Rayu. He also ordered that a daily stipend of one ("Nayudi honnu") piece of gold, levied on the customs, should be allowed to Sidda Rāmapa;* directing Bettada Rao to continue to [the fallen laird] the lands which he used to cultivate under the tank.

15. [Narasappaiia] also appointed Pedda Ramapa Nayu (son of Sidda Ramapa Nayu) with some of his men to serve in the army. His third son Siddappa Nayu was sent away to Sri-Ranga-Patnam [Seringapatam]. And he placed guards over the (Dora) baron to prevent his ever coming out of the mansion. Then [Narsappaiia] himself returned to Gutti.

The second of his sons, named Ramappa Junior, who had previously gone [and taken service in] Hyder's† army, and Ramapa Senior lost their lives in battle.

After a while Narasappiia lost his command, and Tippoo Sultan sent Chistiyar Khan Saheb to manage Gutti: sending Mohammed Ashraf Saheb to rule Handeh Anantapuram: and Husen Khan the Eunuch to command the fort. They on coming sequestrated (zabt) the thirty pagodas per month formerly granted [as a pension] by Narasappa on the taxes [to the fallen baron] and his private cultivation and exercised authority over the country.

---

* In the Fifth Report on the Affairs of the Company, Appendix, page 839 is a note, by *Munro*, (afterwards Governor of Madras) of this person's father. 'His peshcush was reduced by the Mahrattas to 18,000 Rs: in addition to which he paid a chout to Morari Row of 5000 Rs. In 1775 Hyder raised his peishcush to C. Pag. [Kanthiraya Pagodas] 23,625. In 1783 he was sent by Tippoo to Seringapatam as a prisoner.

† Hyder is always designated "The Bahauder" and his son Tippoo is always called "The Sultan;" the real name of neither being, in general, specified. Thus a 'Bahādari honnu' is a gold coin issued by Hyder.

16. After a while these (amaldār) Managers were dismissed, and instead, there were sent, from Seringapatam, Niyāmat Khan to command the fort, and Fatteh Saheb to superintend. These two came and carried on business. As [the poor baron] Sidda Ramappa Nayu was in distress for want of money he sold the clothes, vessels, &c., (*) which, he had by him, and so struggled on. As he was seized with illness, and as he had heard that his two sons Ramapa senior and Ramapa junior were slain in the army, and as the youngest son who had been with him, Siddapa Nayudu, was gone a captive to Seringapatam, and as his crowned wife the lady Caliānamma had died, all these griefs bowed him down so that he pined, and died in the year Kilaca, month Kartica, on the day of the full-moon SS. 1710 [13th Nov. 1788.]

CHAPTER EIGHTH.

1. Afterwards, during the rule of Niyamat Khan and Fatih Saheb, Siddaramappa N.'s sons named Hanumappa, N. and Basavappa N. and the sons of his eldest son Pedda Ramapa N. viz. Sidda Ramappa and Vasanta Rayal, and the (Amma garu) lady mother and others were [alive]: [the Musulmans] put all these persons in guard*. After a few days, Niyamat Khan of the fort was dismissed, and Mēer Khasim was placed instead. He secured the various guards. Then an order arrived from Tippoo Sultan, directing that the commandant of the fort and the manager should bring offerings for the Bakreed festival. Thereupon [Kasim] placed Sayad Husen, the second in command, to rule the fort; while he himself with the (Serishtadars) superintendents proceeded to Seringapatam. There they paid their respects to Tippoo, who said to Mīr Khasim the commandant of the fort, "what is the meaning of your neglecting to obey the command I formerly sent you, directing that two hundred men (belonging to Timma N. of Bengalur, who were on guard

---

(*) Page 63.

* In translating, I use stops, but in the original the whole is one long sentence.

at Anantapuram) should be sent to my presence. To this, Mir Khasim represented "We left them there, [as they were required] for guards to secure Anantapuram, and the prisoners, and the people of the household."

2. On (a) hearing this, Tippoo said, "Are there any more of the family?" Mir Khasim the commandant of the fort replied, "There are Sidda Ramapa N.'s two sons, and two grandsons, and some (amma garlu) ladies: and some sons-in-law and others." On hearing all this, Tippoo Sultan replied, as soon as you return to Anantapuram hang up all the elder sons, and sons-in-law* and send the rest of the people to my presence in Seringapatam.

Mir Khasim took leave and returned to Anantapuram. According to these orders, he hanged up on hooks Hanumappa and Basavappa (sons of Sidda Ramappa) and his son-in-law named Dal Prabhaiia: [this was done at] the first tree in the grove at [the chapel of saint] Kasi Visweswara, twelve miles from Anantapuram: it is on the north side of the village on the west of the road leading to Bucca Raya Samudram:† besides, there being some other people connected with them, named Sāntappa, and Hal Sarabhappa the (dalavai manager) and Subbarayappa junior; these three he hung on a mango tree in Saint Nilamma's grove. He at once put their two grandsons, and others of their kinsfolk, and the mother, under a guard, and sent them to Seringapatam. Thus the family here was ruined.

3. Tippoo Sultan appointed Siddappa N. at Seringapatam, at the rate of sixty Kanthirai pagodas a month wages to superintend two thousand labourers: after conferring this employ on him [Tippoo]

(a) Page 64.

* This resembles the cruel execution of the sons of Saul told in the 21st chapter of the second book of Samuel.

† This sentence is a good specimen of *countermarching.* The words in the original stand in this order. 'Mir Khasim having taken leave, having come to 'Anantapuram; according to the order, Sidda Ramapa N.'s sons Hanumappa 'and Basavappa, son-in-law Dāl Prabhaiia, these three, on the north of the 'village, beyond six coss, to Bucca Raya Samudram, going road, westwards, 'Kasi Visweswar's grove in, first tree on, he on hooks caused to hang.'

had given him suitable officers, and had caused him to build "Nasrat-ābād* in the neighbourhood of Mysore."

But when Siddappa N. heard of all the [cruel murders] that had happened at Anantapuram, he feared lest he himself should suffer, and while he was thinking on this, a friend of his, named Timmana Boyu, who was among those who had come from Anantapuram in order to build Nasratabad, wished to get his son married, and going to the (daroga) overseer, he said 'I here have no kinsfolk: my people who are in the land of Gutti have written to me to come, saying they will bestow a girl [on my son]. I now wish to take leave, and as soon as the marriage is completed, I will return here. (a)

The overseer went to the presence of Tippoo Sultan and stated this request. So he gave Timmana Boi (Kharch-ku) money for his journey, and gave him (rahdari) a passport to take his goods &c.; and so sent him away. When this man [lit. ipse] originally came to this country, Siddappa Nayudu had said [to him] when you go home [to my father's estate] if you will carry me with you and leave me in [my father's] country I will reward you well. To this proposal [Timmana] had consented and given his promise. Accordingly he [secretly] conveyed Siddappa Nayudu with him and having shewn the guards the passport, he went off with the carts carrying his property. After this party had gone ten miles, just after sunrise, Timmana gave one of his men to Siddappa and told him to start and travel with the utmost speed. And Siddappa Nayudu set out and fled for his life, travelling night and day, without halting any where: he went at the rate of [five amadas] fifty miles a day: thus in four days [Siddappa] arrived at home in his estate. Meantime Timmana Boi travelled slowly by easy stages.†

4. Afterwards Siddappa, proceeded to Pāpā Nayuni peta‡ in the Kalahasti country: and after resting there for four days, he bought

---

* Tippoo generally conferred Musulman names on Hindu towns. All the new names perished with him.

(a) Page 65.

† This paragraph is obscure, the words here marked with brackets being omitted.

‡ Most of these names have meanings, Pāpa is an ancient Telugu word for a snake: and Papa Nayu, (Phani-pati) the Dragon king.

a horse, and took ten men into his service and assumed a dignity befitting one in authority. Thence he went to [the town of] Kalahasti,* and halted outside the town, and sent a message by the guards to Damerla Timma Nayu [baron of that place] saying 'Siddappa Nayu, son of Sidda Ramapa N. of Hande Anantapuram, is come to obtain an interview with your honour.' They went and reported the matter to their ruler. He heard them, and on learning that the heir of a noble house had come to visit him, Timma Nayu came forth to meet and greet him. He conducted his guest into a temporary dwelling. Then he [respectfully] took leave and went into his mansion: out of the fort he sent gifts [to his guest] and shewed him every attention. There [he] kept [him] for ten days, bestowing on him gifts of clothing, furniture, &c. and made him a grant of the village named Kunkalāgunta. Then he sent him to Papa-nayuni-peta.(a)

5. This Timma Nayu sent a written order to his (guricādu) agent at that place, stating "This baron is a relation of ours, and you are to pay him every attention, and whatever articles he requires for building a house, you are to procure it, and be very heedful." The agent conducted himself accordingly, and Sidda Nayu built himself a house there. He filled the town, thus given him as a pension, with people,† and carried on tillage on his own account. He dwelt there for five or six years.

The Sultan, the ruler of Seringapatam, who had before carried away from Anantapuram and kept in prison all the family of Siddappa N. took account of their number, and granted them suitable subsistence for six years. But in the year Sadharana [A. D. February 1791] in the month of Magha, the troops of Hara Pant Phatkey attached to the Peshwas‡ and the troops of the Nizam marched through Anantapuram on their way to Seringapatam to besiege it. They caused a great disturbance; and all the petty (Pā-lē-gār) lairds

---

* Those who wish to see Hindu sculpture in perfection may see it at this town.

(a) Page 66.

† A'bād, (Persian) populous.

‡ The *Peshwa* is the title borne by the ruling chieftain among the Marattas. The word Phatkey is said to come from a word meaning Bang! slapdash! and was assumed as the name, or nickname, of a dashing leader.

looked upon this as the proper moment for every man to establish his family, and the people of the remaining states raised forces and committed depredations.

6. Matters standing thus, there was at Rama-durgam a man of the Balija caste, named Rudrapa, of the Lādagonda family : who thought in himself "This is the proper time :" and he went to the village of Paleru [near Anantapur] and spoke thus to the villagers. "I am the son of Sidda Ramapa, laird of Anantapuram : I was the child of a concubine of his. At the time when our little ones were carried off, I escaped, and roamed here and there till I arrived here." Such was his assertion. There was one Chennappa, son of Mogadala Basavappa, a hereditary servant of those lairds : this man joined Rudrappa ; and declared to the townsmen and to all others who asked questions, that this story was true. From his speaking thus they fancied that this very possibly might be the fact. They had him shaven and bathed and sent for vestments &c. which they bestowed on him. They summoned the people and troops from the neighbouring villages and said, "As this personage is the son of our former laird, ([a]) if we make over these villages to him, we may thus extricate ourselves from our present difficulties."

Accordingly they delivered to him the villages of Koracolla and Kūdēru with their dependencies : and garrisoned them for him. They thus installed Rudrappa as their ruler and placed him at Kūdēru. Afterwards a captain named Nayac Bāvā came and garrisoned Rāyadurgam. And one Aswattha Raya, (son of Narsinga Rao, who built the village of Havaliga,) came with Nayac Bava and humbly said to him "My ancestors were the builders of this village :" thereupon Nayac Bava gave up that village to Aswattha Raya.

7. Afterwards, the rogues* who were with Rudrapa at Kuderu, said to him "why should we sit still ? There are many villages to the east of Anantapuram, let us go and man† them all. He replied

---

(a) Page 67.

* 'Dushta chatushtayam' the rascally pack.

† Thana veyu, to garrison, here means to conquer, and then to fill with troops. To '*settle*,' (bandobast cheyu) generally denotes to *plunder*. In the Marata Memoirs of Hyder, which I translated, the same phrase is used.

"We have not either money or men. If we merely run about from place to place what will be the result?" These rogues then took Rudrapa with them, and went to the village of Havaligeh, where they procured an interview between him and Aswaddha Raya: to whom they said "His honour Sivappa, of Hirehal [originally] befriended our family (see chapter V. 3.) And to this day we keep a lamp lighted to his memory. As a similar occasion has now befallen us, if you will now aid our laird Rudrapa with horse and foot, we will carry our own people also, and garrison Anantapuram and settle it. We will thus gain glory to you." So saying they presented to Aswattha Rayu such vessels and vestments as they had brought with them, and [further] held out hopes to him, that if the affair succeeds they would bestow Kūdēru and Korucolla upon him.

8. On hearing these words the Rayu bestowed on them one hundred horse, some gunpowder and bullets, gave Rudrapa a robe of honour and dismissed him. He took from thence his own troops and these horses and seized on the towns of Buccapatnam, Kotta cheru, [New tank] Onticonda [i. e. Lone-hill] and Malle conda [Jessamine-hill] and Marūru, and Muctāpuram [Pearl-town] and other places. He halted in the suburbs of Anantapuram which he besieged.(a)

But news of this having reached Tippoo Sultan at Seringapatam he thought that the (pa-le-gār) lairds had determined violently to strengthen their respective villages. He thereupon dispatched some Baidar* horse commanded by Gazi Khan and Maddu Khan, and [his own brother-in-law] Mīr Mīrān, with five hundred horse, under the orders of his secretary Babu Rao.† He gave orders that provisions should be supplied to the principal forts:‡ and sent money also for this purpose. On arrival at each fort, they furnished suitable supplies (rastu) at each§ place: then on their way towards Gutti

---

(a) Page 68.

* Baidar, a Kannadi word for a marauder. Hyder was originally a leader of such freebooters. In the manuscript the word is wrongly written Haidar.

† Lit: Babu Rao of the kachehri.

‡ *Gallu:* plural of *gadi*, a fortalice or small castle.

§ Observe the reiteration: *gadi-gadi*, and ā, yā.

they proceeded along the Anantapuram road. They sent word into [this] fort: [the Baidars]* passed from Rāptād, and arrived at Anantapuram at noon: and halted in the plain near Our Lady's Lake.†

9. The troops inside the fort opened the gate of the town, and fell upon [Rudrapa's] troops, [who had taken up their position] in the suburbs. A fight took place: and the Baidar horse moved and came and stood opposite the gates that lead to Rāptād, and to (Upparapalli) Miner's town.

Rudrapa Nayu's troops [who had beset the town], on seeing this [being placed between two fires] lost heart, and quitted their lines.‡ As there was no way for flight many were slain. As there was only a little water in the tank the rest rushed into it and were escaping. Seeing this some of the men from the fort, on one side, and the Baidar forces on the other side, laid hold upon them. [Then Tippoo's captains, viz.] Niyamat khan the (Killadar) commandant of the fort, and Fatteh Mohammad the Aumil (superintendent), these two were observing the fight along the market place, standing near the road that goes to miner's Town, in Potū Ray's plain, on the west of the Tank. While they stood there, [the troops brought the fugitives whom] they placed before them.

The Baidar warriors then asked their captains Gazu khan and Maddu khan what punishment ought to be inflicted on these fugitives. They said, "If we cut off their hands and feet, it will spread our fame greatly." Accordingly Niamatkhan and Fattih Saheb, caused the hands and feet of all their prisoners to be cut off. But Rudrapa made his escape with a few followers.

---

* Three different forces are spoken of: in the original their designations are omitted. This made the description obscure.

† The Amma varu, or Honoured Mother, is usually a phrase for Kali or the goddess of the Small pox.

‡ *Morja* is usually rendered a battery: but may be translated "their lines."

CHAPTER NINTH. (*)

1. Afterwards [Tippoo Sultan] the lord of Seringapatam having made (rāzī) peace, the armies of the Peshwa [of Nagpore] and those of the Nizam [of Hydrabad] departed to their homes. Afterwards Niamat khan and Fattih Mohammad Saheb who had been at Anantapuram, garrisoned all the villages, and pacified the villagers: they took steps for the further extension of cultivation. Tippoo Sultan ruled the land until the end of the month of Magha in the year Kalayucti [SS. 1720. A. D. 8th March, 1799.] The English army then came and besieged Seringapatam: the Nizam Alikhan of Hydrabad sent A'mīn Sāheb, and Raja Roshan Rao, and Mīr A'lam, and other captains, with a few troops, to aid the English. They arrived and besieged the fort [of Seringapatam.] After two months an action took place wherein Tippoo Sultan fought and was slain. The date was the new moon in Chaitra in the year Siddharti SS. 1721; (4th May, 1799.) Thus the town of Seringapatam was captured and garrisoned at that time by the English.

2. This news spread on all sides [through the land.] Hande Siddappa Nayu who was living at Papa Nayuni Peta in the Kalahasti country, (see Chap. VIII. Sec. 4.) set out with his people and journeyed to Vemula and Pulivendala and those quarters. He held communications with Erra Gorla Sitanna, Peda Vencatapati and others: he got some troops from them: and marched from thence to Bucca Patnam and Kotta Cheruvu; but when the people living there heard of this, they said "Our laird has arrived:"—they went out to meet him, and brought him to Cotta Cheruvu, where they lodged him in the monastery of Saint Nidu Mamidi. There he halted a week: he raised some troops from the neighbouring villages: and marched in great force to Rāptād.

Meantime* the Killadar, and the risaladars (lieutenants) and the (bel-tamburas)† and (golandaz) grenadiers and other troops who were in the fort of Anantapuram turned upon the First Captain

(*) Page 69.

* This sentence is obscurely arranged.

† Bell-tents? Tippoo coined several new phrases: of which perhaps this is one.

(Avval Killedar) and Second Captain, and Hanumant Rao and Rama Rao, managers of the(Kandachar) revenue demanding payment of the sums due for wages, for the last three months ever since the siege of Seringapatam(*) began. They cast these persons into prison, and treated them mercilessly; at last they got four hundred pagodas from them.

The Sar-bel* named Abrahim Sharif shared out this money among all the people.

Afterwards, Sidda Ramaya, who had arrived at Rāptād, being in the habit of riding (for pleasure) around Anantapuram, was (one day) fired at from the battery and thereupon fled.

3. At this time Vasanta Raya (son of Siddappa Nayu's elder brother) came with his mother and other persons, to Rāptād: having been set free from the dungeons in Seringapatam. Siddappa Nayu embraced Vasanta Raya, evinced much emotion (paschāt tapam) and comforted him. People brought news that [Seringa] patam† had fallen, and that Tippoo Sultan was dead. Thereupon the risaladars at Anantapuram demanded their pay for two months: and also food and clothing for the future: declaring that if these requests were granted they would surrender the town. They sent this message by respectable men to Sidda Ramaya at Rāptād.‡

On hearing it he granted their request. He therefore sent to Anantapuram Lad khan (subadar of Hamlet-on-rock) and Khali Saheb, and Kotappa son of Naga Lingappa. These men came and sat down at the chapel of St. Basawappa in the suburbs: they sent for the risaladars and other respectable men, who were in the fort; and said to them, "as soon as you surrender this fort to us, we will give you the two months wages: and will entertain all your men in our troops: and will pension all four of you." They used many such arguments.

(*) Page 70.

* Probably this means the captain. It seems to be one of the new phrases coined by Tippoo Sultan: such novel expressions abound in the documents framed by him and his servants: which are therefore not easy to explain.

† The word *Patnam*, or Capital is used for Seringapatam, for Madras and for Nagpore.

‡ This paragraph though clear enough in the original has been *countermarched* to make it intelligible in English.

4. The men listened and consented: the two parties conversed together over the matter: and accordingly accepted the tāmbūlam from each other. [The risaladars] said, If you will desire the laird to come as far as Saint Kalianamma's well, and then send word to us in the fort, we will be ready and will come to Basava's-bank, and you(*) and we will go on together and wait upon Him (the laird) and bring him along and deliver the fort [into his hands]. After saying this [the risaladars] returned into the fort. Afterwards, Cotappa and Ladkhan and Khāli Saheb sent a message to the laird telling him these tidings. He was well pleased: and next day he set out from Raptad with his people and came to *Kalianamma's Well.*

When [he] sent word of this into the fort, the Risaladars came forth with some infantry and principal men, and proceeded to Basava's-bank: they brought Cotappa, Ladkhan and Khali Saheb along with them, and went to meet him; [they] offered gifts and honours to Siddappa [their master,] and brought him, with both troops, into Anantapuram, the keys, seals, &c., of which fort they delivered to him: they surrendered the fort to him. After this Siddapa Naik also placed his guards over the 'battery' at the ditch of outer (alangam) circumvallation. Then he bestowed vests on the four (risaladars) captains in the fort, with tāmbūlams, and dismissed them. Then they all retired to their homes.

5. Then, as Siddappa Nayu had not hitherto been married, having settled that the 5th day of the dark fortnight of the month Jeshta, in the year Siddharti [A. D. 22nd June 1799,] would be a suitable time for the wedding, and having made every necessary preparation, he married Nilamma, daughter of Kūsappa of the Zaggula family, who were his kinsmen.

Then Amin Saheb, and Raja Roshan Rao, servants of the Nizam A'li Khan, who had come to Seringapatam to give aid [to the English], were marching with their troops [back into their own country] by the Gurramconda route: they came to Gutti: and in order to garrison and secure it they came on by Anantapuram, and summoned Siddappa Nayu to an interview: they said, "Our Master commands you to de-

---

(*) Page 71.

liver your fort to us: you and your people shall be supplied with food." So they garrisoned Anantapuram, sending [him] and his family to Siddarama puram near Buccapatnam. They gave him this village as subsistence;* and settled that he should also receive ten Pagodas in every hundred. They committed Anantapur to the care of Vencatadri Pantulu (a) The fort was entrusted to one Benacappa, a bramin of the district of A'davāni. Then the troops retired.

6. Afterwards, one Naganatha Rayu was sent by Mīr A'lam, from his district, to rule Anantapuram and some other districts: while he ruled this country, he allowed Siddappa Nayu, to enjoy the village of Sidda Ramapuram for ten months and also ten per cent. [of the revenue], as had been determined by Amin Sahīb.†

Afterwards, Colonel Munro‡ who was attached to *the Company*, sent Narasinga Rao from Kampli and that neighbourhood to settle the district of Anantapuram. He arrived at the village on the sixth of the bright fortnight in Margasira in the year Raudri [i. e. 22nd November 1800.] He settled all the district.

A month after the lands and allowance granted to Siddappa were sequestrated, Tirumalaiia of Maddagirī, was appointed manager and Siva Ramaia was appointed Serishtadar. They came and examined into the accounts and documents concerning this district. And his honour the Colonel himself arrived at Dharmavaram with a view to settle the revenue. He sent for the Seristadār and the Amaldārs and the villagers in these districts, and came to an understanding (chukāya) about the (jumabandi) revenue. Then Hande Siddappa Nayu who was at Siddarama puram came to Dharmavaram, and visited the Colonel, and stated all his history.

7. His honour the Colonel listened to his statement and said 'come along with me and present yourself at Hande Anantapu-

---

* *Ummaligeh:* உம்பிளிக்கை, a field granted rent free, in consideration of the performance of certain services: மானியம். See Rottler's Tamil Dictionary.

(a) Page 72.

† The intricacy of this sentence in the original is observable. The following pages, written in a fluent colloquial style, abound with instances of an inverted syntax: thus being somewhat intricate.

‡ Subsequently Sir Thomas Munro, Governor of Madras. His name is in Kannadi usually spelt Mundrolu. And he is also known as *Colonel Saheb*.

ram.' Accordingly he came to that place with him, and there waited on Munro Saheb: who desired him to state and present his whole story in writing. Accordingly he made four of the oldest farmers sit down, and also Sinappa the vakil of Newtank, and Balappa, and Narasappa of the Vamanna family, and Timmanna (desai) the head man and Venganna and others. They wrote out and gave the entire history.(a) Then his honor Munro Saheb pitying him assigned 75 Canth'erāi pagodas per month, for his stipend, and sequestrated Siddarama Puram near Buccaputnam and its hamlets which were formerly given to him as a Jaghir by Amin Saheb, in the service of the Moguls; as well as the fees that had been allowed him in every village and [instead] he gave him (as stated above) a monthly stipend, and granted an order on the treasury that the money should be paid to his (raseed) 'receipt;' giving him also a (parwana) written order to this effect, directed to the (amildar) Superintendent.

He thus received a monthly allowance, and supported all his dependents.

His wife Nilamma bore a daughter named Changalamma, who was a year old when this Siddappa Nayudu died at Sidda Rama Puram, on the 5th day of the dark fortnight of the month Ashadha, in the year Durmati [SS. 1723, or, 30th July 1801 A. D.]

8. Siddappa Nayu's elder brother's son Vasanta Rayu was twenty years of age when he went to Colonel Munro's camp at Cuddapa; and having waited on him, and stated all his story in writing, [the Colonel] attended [to his statement], but had some doubt, because he had never heard Siddappa Nayu say that his elder brother had a son. Naranappa, the (desai) head man of Dharmavaram, was then in the (hoozoor) Presence as a (munshi) secretary.

This man and Pullappa, son of Sanjivappa, who was the (maniam) superintendent of the customs at Anantapuram, and Sheshaya, son of Pariki Subbanna, these men having gone [to Colonel Munro] for the purpose of contracting for the taxes of the above district, were in [His] Presence. Then Çandi Vencat Rayu and Rama Chandra Raya, the Ministers, and the (Munshis) Secretaries and others who were in the (kacheri) office enquired of Pullappa and Seshappa

---

(a) Page 73.

because they were inhabitants of Anantapuram [concerning this matter.] [They] gave their evidence of all the particulars of the history formerly given in writing: they declared that this Vasanta Rayu was indeed the son of Pedda Ramapa Nayudu, son of Sidda Ramapa the hereditary laird.* And they declared that if this were "more or less" [than the truth] they would suffer any punishment([a]) which the Sircar (Government) might ordain. They executed a (muchilca) bond to this effect to the "Company."

9. Besides Narayanappa the (Desai) head man of Dharmavaram (the other district,)† likewise executed a (muchilka) bond to this effect. Thereupon [the Colonel] appointed that the pension which was granted to Siddappa Nayu should be continued to Vasanta Rayu. He also granted (sannad) an order on the Treasury, of the same purport, to Madhava Rayu the Ameen; then Vasanta Rayu took leave of the Colonel and returned to Siddarama Puram.‡ In a few days after, hearing that the Colonel had gone [lit: *come*] to Anantapuram, this Vasanta Rayu thought of again going to visit him and to request a [peshgi] loan for the purpose of defraying his wedding expenses. He [therefore] came in person to the (Hazur) Court and made his request. [The Colonel] took his request (Khatir-Ku)§ into consideration granting an order on the treasury for an advance of four months' pay.

10. Then, Vasanta Rayu took this sum and provided all that was required for the wedding‖. He married Calyanamma, a girl aged

---

* Lit; *crowned* laird.

([a]) Page 74.

† Parāi tālūca; meaning Dharmavaram.

‡ In translating we are obliged to put semi-colons, or full stops, where the Telugu phrase is "by its being so." Or else, as here shewn "in a few days after he returned;" where English composition would place a full stop.

§ This narrative abounds in Hindustani phraseology, especially in the latter part. Few of the Telugus ever learnt Hindustani or Persian, but until the year 1810 or 1820 it was the favourite study among Bramin officials: though they never attained to a correct pronunciation. At present, in 1850, Hindustani phraseology has gone out of fashion, and English expressions are in vogue: even among those who can neither read nor speak English.

‖ The following lines are countermarched.

nine years, daughter of Nabi Gaudu, of the family of Bāladahanumappa Naik at Sancanahallu, a village in the (pargana) district of Bagavada in the Nijapuram division. This he did after ascertaining the connection of the ancestors: and also Veramma, a girl of nine years old daughter of Karihuli Kottūrappa in the village of Nimbacallu. To these two he was married at the same time.

Vasantarayu died within three months after [these weddings] in the month Jeshta in the year Dundubhi [SS. 1724, that is in June 1802.]

11. Here follows an account of the ladies (amma-gārlu) and others who were afterwards at Siddaramapuram, viz.

Chennamma-garu* is at Coracodu: she is the wife of Ramapa, junior; he is the son of Ponnamma, the junior wife of [the late] Sidda Ramapa Nayudu.

While the late Vasanta Rayu was (ābālyam-yandu) in mere childhood he lost his mother and father, and as she had no son, [the lady Chennamma] took this boy into her bosom and brought him up most tenderly, partaking of all his joys and sorrows. In [Tippoo's] prison at Seringapatam she took care of him, and reared him with extreme fondness: then when his days ended and he departed, she was in deep affliction,(a) and remained for two months in her chamber. The rest of the ladies, namely Sacramma and Nilamma, with Basavappa Nayu's wife [that is, widow, named] Chennamma, senior, and Chennama junior, and some other personages, namely, Sinappa the (vakeel) representative, and Bālappa, and Appanna, of Raghavappa's family, and Vāmanna's [son] Narasappa, and their father confessor (guru), his reverence Basava Lingam of Muttenapandeh, and also "Black"† Basavappa of A'lamūri, and Vīrappa senior, of Nabīrī: these and others, [indeed] all the people, beholding Chennamma sunk in this grief for her son, said to her, "However long you

---

* Garu: literally they: the honorific plural of the pronoun: This (gauroo) added to any name is a mere title of honour. Thus, Amma, mother: but Amma-garu, his lady-mother.

(a) Page. 75.

† Cari: that is black: meaning dark complexioned: while Erra, red, denotes Fair, or tawny.

indulge grief regarding the doings of Providence, it is of no avail. The dead are utterly departed [lit. going they are gone]. You should look to the well-being of those now living.*

12. "You sent for these [two] girls from a place three or four hundred miles distant, and married [them to him]. Now consider the state [to which they are reduced]. During the two months which you have now passed lying in a corner, in deep affliction, who is there to manage the family? You should pluck up heart: there is much to be done. You should state all these things to the Colonel, and act according to his advice."

So saying they pressed and counselled her much, and comforted and advised her.† Then the lady Nila and lady Sacra, by means of some respectable men, wrote and sent a message to lady Chenna, stating that they awaited her commands, declaring that they would be guided by her wishes.

Lady Chenna, yielding in some measure to their letters, directed Sīnappa the above mentioned agent (vakil), and Balappa, and Nabīri Vīrappa, and others to set out on a journey: they went (lit. having come) to Anantapuram, where they narrated all the story to ("Mandrolu Saheb") Colonel Munro: he listened to it, and said 'which of these ladies is a person of sufficient sense, to manage the family?' Then all (lit. ten) joined in making a request, in writing, that Dame Chenna should be appointed as the head of the family. The Colonel listened to the request. He ordered that money should be advanced

* We see the emptiness and misery of Hinduism chiefly when a death occurs. The Hindus have no hope in death: there is a miserable glimmering notion about the fruit of (pūrva janmam) a former birth, and with a strange refinement in cruelty they (sometimes) curse a miserable widow assuring her that her sins in a former birth have occasioned the death of her husband. Their ideas regarding a future life are all darkness and doubt. The idea of transmigration is often in their mouths and perpetually occurs in their books, regarding *past* time: but does not seem to be clearly believed regarding the future. The future well being of the deceased is imagined to depend on the due performance of monthly and annual funeral rites. In its practical effects Hinduism is all delusion, and especially as regards a future life the Hindus appear to be devoid of all hope.

† Here is no allusion to the burning or burying of widows alive. That custom probably ceased after the Musulman rule began.

(peshgi) to him to meet the expenses attending the days of mourning for Vasanta Rao. He issued an order on the treasury to this effect.

13.([a]) The (vakeels) ambassadors replied "There is no [representative] for this family, for the future.* When they originally came here from Bijapuram, some of the family remained there." The messengers then presented a statement saying "We look for your honour's permission, and wish to send for some young son of the house, from thence, and crown him [as heir]." Colonel Munro attended to their statement, and gave permission accordingly.

Then the (vakils) messengers returned to Siddarámapuram,† and reported all this to Dame Chenna and the other Lady-mothers, and to Nabī Gaudu (the father-in-law of the late Vasanta Rayu) and to the other personages there; they listened, and [said] to the messengers. "In the Bagavadi division, in the Nijapuram country, there was Lakki Nayacu, of the two villages Muttigeh, and Vadavadigi; he was the (mula purusha) head of the family: he had two sons named Bālada Hanumappa Nayukudu, and Balaga Nayacudu. The descendants of Balada Hanumappa formerly came to Bellary and Anantapuram, and thereabouts. Balaga Nayak's descendants remained "there" [that is, in the Nijapuram country]. The particulars are recorded on the tombs of the Handeh family,‡ and in other places: it is the truth: we have seen it." They then sent (with these messengers) Cari Basavappa; (of A'lamūru) and (a Jangam priest) named Siva Linga Devāra at the Buccapatnam convent: and Chinna Rāmanna of the Nagari country: and Gidda Mallappa: and Kottigeh Basavappa: and Peda Kōtappa:§ and others, [z] with instructions to bring the little fellow there.

These persons therefore set out and went to the abovesaid (sadar)

([a]) Page 76.

* Lit: *mundu*, that is, Before. Here again is an instance of the words *Before* and *After*, changing senses.

† It should be Sidda Rama Puram.

‡ Gummatam (from the Persian *gunbaz*, a dome) and *Samadhi* a tomb. The persons here named, as is specified below, were Lingajangams: a sect who bury their dead.

§ In the original the word "one" is added to each name, as is usual in lists.

villages. On seeing the proofs pointed out by Nabi Gaudu and other personages, they selected a boy named Sidda Ramapa, of the descendants of Balaga Nayak and brought him away.

14. They placed* this child on the lap of Lady Kalyani, the wife of [the late] hereditary laird Vasanta Nayu; she accepted him as her adopted son† and reared him. But some vile persons [went and told] lady Nilamma [saying] lady Chenna is bringing up a son: there now appears no prospect of your obtaining any authority [lit. thy world]. Thou art not so helpless [a-tantru-ralu] as to be under the dominion of Lady Chenna.(a) It will therefore be best that a division of the property should be made and that thou shouldst part from her and live independently.

Such was their counsel. The lady assented. When the (vakil) agent came to Anantapuram and carried away the money, for the pension, Lady Nila's younger brother and others, her partisans came, and arrested him. The money remained untouched in the (kachehri) office. Then lady Chenna's agents, and those employed by Lady Nila, went to the (hazoor) presence [of Colonel Munro] where there was a (Panchayat) jury assembled: which sat for two or three months: and a decision was made in the presence [to this effect.]

"Lady Chenna shall have two (hissa) shares: and Lady Nila and Lady Sacra shall have, as their two (roosooms) pensions, one (hissa) share; total three shares:" thus the (sambalam) subsistence was granted. An order (perwana) to this effect was (sadir) issued to Narasing Rao the superintendent of the abovesaid district: and thus was the decision made.

And the evidence regarding this is his honour the Colonel's (parwana) grant.

15. Afterwards: Lady Chenna's house was broken into by thieves and all her property was carried off. And as there was a dispute

---

* Lit: By placing.

† Here again is an instance shewing that the rules laid down by Menu and other authorities were not observed. According to them adoption must be made by the husband and the wife: not by the survivor. No widow can adopt a son, under the Braminical laws. But these people being Lingavants, (Jangams) disregard those laws.

(a) Page 77.

between her and Lady Nila, she entertained (andesha) apprehensions fearing lest any harm should happen to the [adopted] lad. His honour (hazrat) the Colonel was then in the Pulivendula country, she sent (vakils) her agents thither to declare that [Lady Chenna] was not content (rāzī) to dwell in Sidda Rama Puram; and that if permitted she would go and live at the village Coracodu in the same district, where she proposed to build a house. They presented her petition to this effect. His honour (khāvind) assented and ordered that she should be granted a place at her selection in Coracodu. He gave a written authority to this purport, to Narsinga Rao the (āmīn) superintendent; who accordingly sent for the head farmers and clerks of Coracodu, and directed that two houses should be granted [to her]. They therefore allotted a place for [building] two houses; and [she] laid out two-hundred pagodas,* in building a palace, and caused a draw-well to be dug;† and quitting Siddarama Puram she came and dwelt at Cora-cōdu.

16. ([a]) Then with a view to obtaining a ratification regarding this boy, Sidda Ramapa Nayudu, as Colonel Munro was encamped at Adavani (Adhoni) the Lady Chenna, and Sidda Ramapa Nayu, and the agents and others went [to wait on Colonel Munro]. But his honour left that place and halted near Vreshtapādu in the Guttī division: so they went there, and had an interview; when [the lady] stated thus "When we formerly presented a petition at Anantapuram, we received your honour's commands: according to which we have brought the little fellow." He listened to the whole statement, and replied with the greatest kindness, saying, "Bring up this boy." They took leave and returned well pleased to Coracodu.

Subsequently, after his honour the Colonel went to (Vilait) England, Mr. Travers came, who settled Codiconda [literally, made it a zilla.] And after his honour departed, Mr. Gahagan came and performed the duty of Collector. The Vakeels before mentioned brought his honour Sidda Ramapa Nayudu, whom the Lady Chenna

---

* According to the reckoning of those days, eight hundred Rupees.

† Chēduta is to draw water with the hand: and a *chēdu bavi*, or draw well, is small, as compared with the enormous wells common in that country.

([a]) Page 78.

had reared, to Anantapuram, and caused him to have an interview with (Hazrat varu) his honour. They stated the particulars of the Colonel's commands: and the substance of what he condescended to say: the interview with him that took place in Camp at Gooty: all these things. Then His Honour too [that is, Mr. G.] gave similar directions.

17. Afterwards, as they [The Laird and the agents] were coming home, they arrived at Saint Basava's chapel [at Anantapuram,] and offered him homage. Then they marched in state around the town with the Umbrella, the chauris, and yellow robe, and [all other royal] insignia, accompanied by the songs of heralds; they again arrived at the place where they had halted.

Then they [all] remained in Anantapuram five or six days. Then [the agents] took leave of their Master [Dhani, meaning Mr. G.] and arrived at home in Coracodu.

After a short time* (9)they sent for a maid (8)named Lingamma, a girl (7)five years old. (6)daughter of (5)Jaggula Sacrappa (4) who had long been allied with the family (3) and who lived (2) at a village called Gallu(1) in the Gutti division. They duly delivered the *tambulam* as a testimonial, and betrothed her as wife to Sidda Ramappa, according to the rules of the caste, and the observances of the family. They brought the little girl, and lodged her in the mansion, and to this day they are tending her.

18. He lives there until the present time: that is, the year named Prajōtpatti, the month Vaishāka full moon, in the crescent, [that is, 8th May 1811.]

The following are the usages of the Handeh family. They are adorers of Siva; and wear the Lingam.† The hereditary god, and patron saint they worship is Sidda Rameswarudu of Sonnalāpuram: in the Bijāpoor country. They adore no other saints. They do not

---

* This sentence is a good instance of the *countermarching* which often makes the colloquial Telugu deviate so greatly from English.

† An Essay on the Manners and Customs of the Vira Saivas, or, Jangams was printed by me in the Madras Journal, in the year 1840.

drink water unless they have first adored Siva. They eat sweet food, but never use flesh or spirits. They contract marriages with no girl who has grown up. When the term of life is over, and they die, they are duly interred according to the Vira Saiva rites.

THE END.